Honey,
1998

You are a wonderful father to our
Don. May this book enrich your
life and bring you close to
your heavenly father.
Happy fathers
Day
Honey!!
Your wife

15 Minutes

ALONE
WITH GOD
FOR MEN

Bob Barnes

D0061784

HARVEST HOUSE PUBLISHERS
Eugene, Oregon 97402

Cover by Terry Dugan Design, Minneapolis, Minnesota.

15 MINUTES ALONE WITH GOD FOR MEN

Copyright © 1995 by Harvest House Publishers
Eugene, Oregon 97402

Library of Congress Cataloging-in-Publication Data

Barnes, Bob, 1933-
    15 minutes alone with God for men/Bob Barnes.
        p.   cm.
    ISBN 1-56507-325-8
    1. Men—Prayer-books and devotions—English.   I. Title.   II. Title: Fifteen
minutes alone with God for men.
BV4843.B37   1995
242'.642—dc20   94-44254
                                                     CIP

97 98 99 00 01 02 03 / BC / 15 14 13 12 11 10 9 8 7

This book is dedicated to the various pastors, coaches, businessmen, and fellow journeyers who have contributed to my Christian walk. Though they are far too many to mention by name, I have been blessed through the years by their guidance, love, and example.

I especially want to dedicate this devotional to my son Bradley and his son Bradley Joe II and my son-in-law Craig and his sons Chad and Bevan Merrihew. These five males certainly contribute to the goodness of my life. May they all stay near to God so that He can impact their lives in a mighty way.

15 Minutes Alone with God

As we enter the last part of the '90s, God is at work among men in America in a mighty way. More and more men are hearing and responding to His call to be leaders in the family and the church. Many men are naming Jesus their Lord and Savior for the first time, and others are rededicating themselves to the Lord. If these commitments are to make a significant impact in our families, our nation, and our world, they need to be nourished daily, and that, I pray, is where this book comes in.

One way we sustain our commitment to the Lord is to read His Word daily. The material in this devotional is designed to challenge and encourage men in their spiritual journey by getting them into God's Word. In each of the following 15-minute entries, you'll read a passage in Scripture and a short devotion based on that selection, pray about what you've read, and then be challenged to act on what you've learned.

Don't worry about reading the book from front to back. Skip around if you like. In the upper right-hand corner on the first page of each entry, you'll find three boxes. Put a checkmark in one of the boxes each time you read it. In this way, you can keep track of those devotions which you have read previously. But keep in mind that, if you consistently spend 15 minutes a day for several weeks, you'll be on the way toward a lifelong habit of spending a few moments alone with God every day.

May the Lord richly bless you as you listen for and respond to His call to you to be a leader in your family, your church, and your community.

— Bob Barnes
Riverside, California

Becoming Involved
with God

    You can read about him in the creeds and in books of theology, or you can get to know God by becoming involved with him, by arguing with him like Job, by wrestling with him like Jacob, by praying to him like Daniel, and by living with him in the desert for forty years like Israel. You can learn about God with your mind or through your experience. God prefers the latter. He wants us to know him experientially, to engage him with our whole lives.

— *John Timmer*

Time for God

Scripture Reading: Psalm 116:1-2
Key Verse: Psalm 116:2b
I will call on him as long as I live.

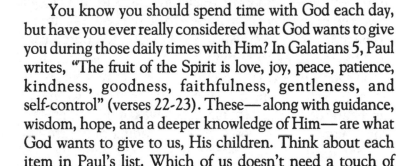

You know you should spend time with God each day, but have you ever really considered what God wants to give you during those daily times with Him? In Galatians 5, Paul writes, "The fruit of the Spirit is love, joy, peace, patience, kindness, goodness, faithfulness, gentleness, and self-control" (verses 22-23). These—along with guidance, wisdom, hope, and a deeper knowledge of Him—are what God wants to give to us, His children. Think about each item in Paul's list. Which of us doesn't need a touch of God's love, patience, kindness, goodness, gentleness, and self-control in our life?

"But," you say, "who has time? My 'To Do' list is always longer than my day. I run from the time the alarm goes off in the morning until I fall into bed at night. How can I possibly find time to do one more thing? When could I find even a few minutes to read the Bible or pray?" Let me answer your questions with a question. Are you doing what's important in your day—or only what is urgent?

People do what they want to do. All of us make choices, and when we don't make time for God in our day, when we don't make time for the most important relationship in our life, we are probably not making the best choices.

God greatly desires to spend time alone with you. After all, you are His child (John 1:12; Galatians 3:26). He created you, He loves you, and He gave His only Son for your salvation. Your heavenly Father wants to know you, and He wants you to know Him. The Creator of the universe wants to meet with you alone daily. How can you say no to such an opportunity?

I know people who spend hours commuting on the California freeways and use that time to be with God. I used to pray while I was driving an hour between home and work. Now that the children are raised and our home is quiet, I find morning—before the telephone starts to ring or I get involved in the day's activities—to be the best time for me to be alone with God. And I love getting to church early and having 10 or 15 minutes to open my Bible and think upon God's thoughts. Despite the distracting talk that is often going on around me, I use this block of time to prepare my heart for worship. (In fact, I believe if more members of the congregation devoted time to reading Scripture and praying for the service beforehand, church would be more meaningful for every worshiper.) Although the times and places where we meet God will vary, meeting alone with God each day should be a constant in our life. After all, we are God's children and, like any good father, He wants to spend time with us.

"Okay," you say. "You've convinced me. I need to be more regular in my time with God— but exactly what should I do when I'm alone with Him?" I suggest that you read and meditate on God's Word for a while (devotional books like this one can help) and then spend some time in prayer. Talk to God as you would to your earthly parent or a special friend who loves you, desires the best for you, and wants to help you in every way possible. Here are a few suggestions:

- Praise God for who He is, the Creator and Sustainer of the universe who is interested in you, His child (Matthew 10:30).

- Thank God for all He has done for you...for all He is doing for you...and for all that He will do for you in the future (1 Thessalonians 5:16-18).

- Confess your sins. Tell God about those things you have done and said and thought for which you are sorry. Remember that He is "faithful and just and will forgive us our sins" (1 John 1:9) whenever we confess them.

- Pray for your family.... Pray for friends and neighbors who have needs, physical, emotional, or spiritual.... Ask God to work in the heart of someone you hope will come to know Jesus as Savior.... Pray for our government officials...for your minister and church officers...for missionaries and other Christian servants (Philippians 2:4).

- Pray for yourself. Ask for God's guidance in the day ahead. Ask God to help you do His will...and to arrange opportunities for you to serve Him throughout the day (Philippians 4:6).

Time with your heavenly Father is never wasted. If you spend time alone with God in the morning, you'll start your day refreshed and ready for whatever comes your way. If you spend time alone with Him in the evening, you'll go to sleep relaxed, resting in His care, and wake up ready for a new day to serve Him.

Remember, too, that you can talk to Him anytime, anywhere—in school, at work, on the freeway, at home—and about anything. You don't have to make an appointment to ask Him for something you need or to thank Him for something you have received from Him. God is interested in everything that happens to you.

> *Father God, thank You for the privilege of prayer—and forgive me for taking it for granted. I want to spend time with You each day. I want to know You better, and I want You to hear my adoration, my confessions, my thanksgivings, and my supplications. Help me to live according to this desire, despite all the demands I feel.... And teach me, Lord, to call on You in every situation throughout the day. Thank You that You are always within the sound of my voice and always only a thought away.... And as I pray, teach me to be genuine with You, unconcerned about eloquence or impressive speech and listening for what You would say to me. Amen.*

Taking Action

❖ If you aren't already spending time with God each day, decide today that you will give it a try for one month.

❖ Tell someone of your commitment and ask that person to hold you accountable.

❖ Read the prayer in Colossians 1:9-12 each day this month.

Reading On

Galatians 5:22-23   Galatians 3:26
John 1:12   Luke 5:16
Matthew 14:23   1 Peter 5:7

Lord, make me an
instrument of your peace!
Where there is hatred,
let me sow love;
where there is injury, pardon;
where there is doubt, faith;
where there is despair, hope;
where there is darkness, light;
and where there is sadness, joy.

O Divine Master,
grant that I may not
so much seek to be consoled
as to console;
to be understood
as to understand;
to be loved
as to love;
for it is in giving
that we receive;
it is in pardoning
that we are pardoned;
and it is in dying
that we are born to Eternal Life.

— *Francis of Assisi*

God's Man for Life

Scripture Reading: Job 1:1-22

Key Verse: Job 1:22

In all this, Job did not sin by charging God with wrongdoing.

———— ❖ ————

A landholder, rancher, and community leader, Job was the most respected and influential individual in the entire region. Still, his number one priority was his large, active family. Despite the tremendous demands on him, he always had time for his children. They were never an interruption. And you couldn't talk to him very long without him pulling from his wallet a favorite picture of his troop. He was always eager to tell you about each of them. This wise man knew that his only legacy of significance would be not his possessions or his bank accounts but his sons, his daughters, and his grandchildren. A man living in the present but with a vision for the future, a man of God, and a man whom God had greatly blessed, Job caught Satan's eye.

In verse 8, as the Lord holds court in the heavenlies, He asks Satan, "Have you considered my servant Job? There is no one on earth like him; he is blameless and upright, a man who fears God and shuns evil."

Satan shrugs his shoulders and replies, in effect, "Of course Job is close with you. Who wouldn't be? He's got all the advantages. You handle him softly and protect him. Just try taking away a few of his precious toys and then see what he does. He'll surely curse you to your face."

For reasons unknown to us, God gives Satan some freedom to do what he wishes most, and that is to test Job's faith. God sets limits, but even within those limits Satan brings great loss and immeasurable pain to Job.

In a quick series of catastrophes, Job loses his business, his wealth, his health, and all ten of his children. At this point, Job's wife tells him to curse God and die (Job 2:9). Finding himself all alone now, would Job remain a man of God or would he reject the God who had once so richly blessed him? Is Job a man of character or a fair-weather follower of God?

Job remained God's man and, by doing so, offers us many valuable lessons for life. One of these lessons is the fact that things on the outside can be taken away from us, but no one can take away those things on the inside—our heart, our character, our soul. We can throw these away by turning from God and following after false gods, but no one can ever rob us of a heart and soul committed to the Lord or of the character that results from that commitment.

So what will you do when the things of life are taken away from you? What will happen to the inner man? Will you stand strong in Christ? Will the loss purify and strengthen your character or break you?

We know that Job's trials strengthened his character, and people talk about the patience of Job. But he demonstrated more than patience. He shows us a faith in God that has staying power and is able to endure to the end. As our key verse says, "Through all of this [his losses and suffering] Job did not sin nor did he blame God." Now turn to Job 42:10-16 and see how our faithful God responds to His people who have faith in Him. May that passage give

———— ❖ ————

you hope when the circumstances of life bog you down. You can rejoice in the Lord in all situations and give thanks whatever challenges come your way, knowing that God is your faithful Redeemer.

> *Father God, thank You for all that You can teach me through the life of Job. Thank You for showing me the importance of faith in You that has staying power. May my life reflect the endurance of Job, whatever comes my way. Help me not measure my life by outward success. Help me to see the internal as much more important and to make choices that preserve the character You are developing in me.*
>
> *I pray that You, merciful God, will spare me from the kind of testing Job underwent. If I am tested, may I find strength in my faith in You. As I trust You with my life, help me to trust that You know what I can handle and that therefore I can handle whatever comes my way. And when the trials are over, I know I will be even more the person You want me to be. Amen.*

Taking Action

❖ List five commitments you have made in your life.
- — How are you doing with them?
- — Which ones fell by the wayside? Why?
- — Are you satisfied with your progress? Why or why not?

❖ Now list your blessings and thank God for each one of them.

❖ Finally, list those areas of your life that are giving you difficulty. Thank God for each because these struggles are the source of spiritual growth.

Reading On

Take a week and read the rest of the book of Job. Turn to this book whenever you feel like you're being teste.d

> I have some dreams. It is time for us as men to reject this fragile male ego business. We use it to cover up our failures and avoid looking at ourselves. Thus the women and children in our lives, who presumably have better egos than we do, must pick up the slack and take responsibility for our actions and feelings. Come on, guys! Let us at least try to struggle honestly. We need to be confronted by our actions, messages and shortcomings if we expect to learn and grow. No more hiding behind excuses. No blaming others. No hiding behind phrases like "This is just the way I am." Let us have a look at who we are, for that is the best indication of who our sons will become.
>
> — *E. James Wilder*

A Man of God...

❖ *Fosters commitment to God through the generations.*
Your faith may result in part from the faith of your father and his. Likewise, your godly example will encourage your children to commit their lives to God.

❖ *Is committed to raising children.*
Despite what our culture says, the quantity of time you spend with your children is as important as its quality.

❖ *Earns the respect of his associates.*
A godly man sets a new standard for doing business as well as for being married and fathering.

❖ *Is a man of mercy.*
Being tough does not mean lacking in compassion, tenderness, or mercy.

❖ *Is a man of justice.*
Knowing what is wrong and not being afraid to respond accordingly, a godly man seeks out truth and acts justly.

❖ *Is stable, not restless.*
Knowing where you are going and going that way with the Lord means stability for you, and it will help give your family purpose and direction as well.

❖ *Is wise.*
Real wisdom is the ability to take God's truth and apply it to life, and a pure man does that.

"I've Sacrificed My Son for You"

Scripture Reading: 1 Peter 1:13-25

Key Verses: 1 Peter 1:18-19

For you know that it was not with perishable things such as silver or gold that you were redeemed...but with the precious blood of Christ....

After you read the following allegory, you'll think differently about the sacrifice God made for you by letting His Son die for your sins....

The time was the Roaring Twenties. The place was Oklahoma. John Griffith was in his early twenties—newly married and full of optimism. Along with his lovely wife, he had been blessed with a beautiful, blue-eyed baby. With delight and excitement, John was dreaming the American dream.

He wanted to be a traveler. He imagined what it would be like to visit faraway places with strange-sounding names. He would read about them and research them. His hopes and dreams were so vivid that at times they seemed more real than reality itself. But then came 1929 and the great stock market crash.

With the shattering of the American economy came the devastation of John's dreams. The winds that howled through Oklahoma were strangely symbolic of the gale force that was sweeping away his hopes. Oklahoma was being systematically ravaged by depression and despair.

And so, brokenhearted, John packed up his few possessions and with his wife and little son, Greg, headed east in an old Model-A Ford. They made their way toward Missouri, to the edge of the Mississippi River, and there he found a job tending one of the great railroad bridges that spanned the massive river.

Day after day John would sit in a control room and direct the enormous gears of an immense bridge over the mighty river. He would look out wistfully as bulky barges and splendid ships glided gracefully under his elevated bridge. Then, mechanically, he would lower the massive structure and stare pensively into the distance as great trains roared by and became little more than specks on the horizon. Each day he looked on sadly as they carried with them his shattered dreams and his visions of far-off places and exotic destinations.

It wasn't until 1937 that a new dream began to be birthed in his heart. His young son was now eight years old, and John had begun to catch a vision for a new life, a life in which Greg would work shoulder-to-shoulder with him, a life of intimate fellowship and friendship. The first day of this new life dawned and brought with it new hope and a fresh purpose. Excitedly they packed their lunches and, arm in arm, headed off toward the immense bridge.

Greg looked on in wide-eyed amazement as his dad pressed down the huge lever that raised and lowered the vast bridge. As he watched, he thought that his father must surely be the greatest man alive. He marveled that his dad could single-handedly control the movements of such a stupendous structure.

Before they knew it, noontime had arrived. John had just elevated the bridge and allowed some scheduled ships to pass through. And then, taking his son by the hand, they headed off for lunch. Hand in hand, they inched their way down a narrow catwalk and out onto an observation deck that projected some 50 feet over the majestic Mississippi. There they sat and watched spellbound as the ships passed by below.

As they ate, John told his son, in vivid detail, stories about the marvelous destinations of the ships that glided below them. Enveloped in a world of thought, he related story after story, his son hanging on every word.

Then, suddenly, in the midst of telling a tale about the time the river had overflowed its banks, he and his son were startled back to reality by the shrieking whistle of a distant train. Looking at his watch in disbelief, John saw that it was already 1:07. Immediately he remembered that the bridge was still raised and that the Memphis Express would be by in just minutes.

Not wanting to alarm his son, he suppressed his panic. In the calmest tone he could muster, he instructed his son to stay put. Quickly leaping to his feet, he jumped onto the catwalk. As the precious seconds flew by, he ran at full tilt to the steel ladder leading into the control house.

Once in, he searched the river to make sure that no ships were in sight. And then, as he had been trained to do, he looked straight down beneath the bridge to make certain nothing was below. As his eyes moved downward, he saw something so horrifying that his heart froze in his chest. For there, below him in the massive gearbox that housed the colossal gears that moved the gigantic bridge, was his beloved son.

Apparently Greg had tried to follow his dad but had

fallen off the catwalk. Even now he was wedged between the teeth of two main cogs in the gearbox. Although he appeared to be conscious, John could see that his son's leg had already begun to bleed profusely. Immediately an even more horrifying thought flashed through his mind. For in that instant he knew that lowering the bridge meant killing the apple of his eye.

Panicked, his mind probed in every direction, frantically searching for solutions. Suddenly a plan emerged. In his mind's eye he saw himself grabbing a coiled rope, climbing down the ladder, running down the catwalk, securing the rope, sliding down toward his son, and pulling him back up to safety. Then in an instant he would move back down toward the control lever and thrust it down just in time for the oncoming train.

As soon as these thoughts appeared, he realized the futility of his plan. Instantly, he knew that there just wouldn't be enough time. Perspiration began to bead on John's brow, terror written over every inch of his face. His mind darted here and there, vainly searching for yet another solution. What would he do? What could he do?

His thoughts rushed in anguish to the oncoming train. In a state of panic, his agonized mind considered the 400 people that were moving inexorably closer toward the bridge. Soon the train would come roaring out of the trees with tremendous speed. But this— this was his son...his only child...his pride...his joy.

His mother— he could see her tearstained face now. This was their child, their beloved son. He was his father and this was his boy.

He knew in a moment there was only one thing he could do. He knew he would have to do it. And so, burying his face under his left arm, he plunged down the lever. The cries of his son were quickly drowned out by the relentless sound of the bridge as it ground slowly into position. With only seconds to spare, the Memphis Express—with its 400 passengers—roared out of the trees and across the mighty bridge.

John Griffith lifted his tearstained face and looked into the windows of the passing train. A businessman was reading the morning newspaper. A uniformed conductor was glancing nonchalantly at his large vest pocket-watch. Ladies were already sipping their afternoon tea in the dining cars. A small boy, looking strangely like his own son, Greg, pushed a long thin spoon into a large dish of ice cream. Many of the passengers seemed to be engaged in either idle conversation or careless laughter.

But no one looked his way. No one even cast a glance at the giant gearbox that housed the mangled remains of his hopes and dreams.

In anguish he pounded the glass in the control room and cried out, "What's the matter with you people? Don't you care? Don't you know I've sacrificed my son for you? What's wrong with you?"

No one answered; no one heard. No one even looked. Not one of them seemed to care. And then, as suddenly as it had happened, it was over. The train disappeared, moving rapidly across the bridge and out over the horizon.

Even now as I retell this story, my face is wet with tears. For this allegory illustration is but a faint glimpse of what God the Father did for us in sacrificing His Son, Jesus, to atone for the sins of the world (John 3:16). However, unlike the Memphis Express that caught John Griffith by surprise, God—in His great love and according to His sovereign will and purpose—determined to sacrifice His Son so that we might live (1 Peter 1:19-20). Not only that, but the consummate love of Christ is demonstrated in that He was not accidentally "caught," as was John's son. Rather, He willingly sacrificed His life for the sins of humankind (John 10:18; cf. Matthew 26:53).[1]

> *Father God, as a father myself, my heart aches as I read today's devotion. It's hard for me to imagine having to make that kind of decision. In a very small way I get a sense of what You, our heavenly Father, had to go through when You sent Your Son to earth to die for our sins. I thank You for making that kind of sacrifice. You are truly a God of endless love. Amen.*

Taking Action

❖ Sit quietly for a few minutes and continue to consider what it means to sacrifice your son so that others may live. What does today's devotional teach you about God the Father? About your fathering?

❖ Spend some time in prayer, thanking God for making the ultimate sacrifice of His only Son for your sins.

❖ Share this story with another father and tell him what it meant to you when you first read it.

Reading On

John 3:16   John 10:18   Matthew 26:53

Abba Father

It was Jesus himself who reminded us that we were to call him Father—"*Abba* Father"—which is a lot more like calling him "Dad." I think Jesus was telling us that our Father is the one in the stands who is standing on the seat, waving his coat in a circle over his head, with tears of pride and happiness running down his face.

— *Bob Benson*

What Your Kids Need to Hear

Scripture Reading: Psalm 127:1-5

Key Verse: Psalm 127:3

> *Sons are a heritage from the Lord, children a reward from him.*

———— ❖ ————

"Oh look, Daddy, I catched it!"

That's my boy. Now get ready; here comes another. Make me proud and catch this one too.

"Look, Daddy, I'm only eight years old and I can throw faster than anyone in the league!"

But your batting stinks, Tiger. Can't play in the big leagues if you can't hit.

"Look, Dad, I'm sixteen and already made the varsity team."

You better do a little less bragging and a little more practicing on your defense. Still need a lot of work.

"Look, Father, I'm thirty-five and the company has made me a vice president!"

Maybe someday you'll start your own business like your old man, then you'll really feel a sense of accomplishment.

"Look at me, Dad. I'm forty, successful, well-respected in the community. I have a wonderful wife and family— aren't you proud of me now, Dad?

24

"All my life it seems I've caught everything but that one prize I wanted most—your approval. Can't you say it, Dad? Is it too much to ask for? Just once I'd like to know that feeling every child should have of being loved unconditionally. I'd like for you to put your arm around my shoulders and, instead of telling me I'm not good enough, tell me that in your eyes I'm already a winner and always will be no matter what.

"Look at me, Daddy. I'm all grown up...but in my heart still lives a little boy who yearns for his father's love. Won't you pitch me the words I've waited for all my life?"

"I'll catch them, Father, I promise." [2]

Do your children know you love them? Do your kids know unconditional acceptance? Are your kids winners in your eyes— and do they know that? Our children need to know that Mom and Dad really love them. They long to hear us say, "I love you and I am very proud of you." And they need to know of our love for them even when they...

- Yell and scream in the grocery store

- Have temper tantrums in the restaurant

- Wear strange clothes

- Have funny haircuts and oddly colored hair

- Use vulgar language

- Run away from home

- Do poorly in school

- Run around with friends that we don't approve of

Often they are using behaviors like these to ask indirectly, "Do you love me?" What are they hearing from your reaction?

A good friend's son was not into sports like his dad desired. Instead, he was into motocross racing. When the parents went to our pastor, the dad asked what he should do. The pastor said, without hesitation and not surprisingly, "Take up motocross!" Predictably, the dad said, "I don't like dirt, grease, motorcycles, the people who ride, sunburns, or the long days at the track." To this, the pastor replied, "Fine— but how much do you love your son? Enough to get grease on your hands and clothes?" The following week our friend was off to the local motocross event with his son. They were soon very involved with dirt, grease, and people our friend would never have chosen to spend his weekend with. But through these actions, this father showed his son that he loved him.

Your children are a gift to you. The psalmist calls them "a heritage from the Lord...a reward from him." What are you doing to show your kids that you love them?

> *Father God, teach me to show my kids that I love them and prompt me to tell them with words, too. Help me be creative, unselfish, and willing to do things with them that aren't my first choice. Raising kids is a tough job, Lord. I need Your help. Amen.*

Taking Action

❖ Write each of your children— whatever their age— a note to let them know how much you love them. Be specific about a few things you love about them.

❖ Plan to spend some quality one-on-one time with each of your children. Ask them what they want to do and then do it!

❖ On next month's calendar, schedule another date with each child.

❖ You might want to share the poem below with your older kids.

Reading On

Psalm 127:3   Proverbs 16:24
Psalm 128:1-3   Proverbs 18:10

You Are You and I Am Me

I hope you know I'm not the person
That I want you to be.
It's important for you to realize
You are you and I am me.
There are faults I have and deeds I've done.
I'd never wish for you.
But those can be your greatest lessons
of what to or not to do.[3]

Unconditional Love

Remember, Son, if you're a success,
I'll be happy as can be.
But remember, too, that when you fail,
You can always come to me.
There's little in life we cannot share.
We'll share the bad times, too,
For my love has no conditions, Son.
That's what I give to you.

— *George E. Young*

Are You Sure You're a Christian?

Scripture Reading: Romans 3:21-31

Key Verses: Romans 3:22-24

> *This righteousness from God comes through faith in Jesus Christ to all who believe. There is no difference, for all have sinned and fall short of the glory of God, and are justified freely by his grace through the redemption that came by Christ Jesus.*

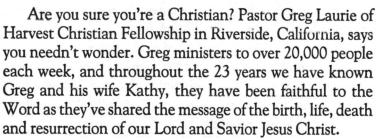

Are you sure you're a Christian? Pastor Greg Laurie of Harvest Christian Fellowship in Riverside, California, says you needn't wonder. Greg ministers to over 20,000 people each week, and throughout the 23 years we have known Greg and his wife Kathy, they have been faithful to the Word as they've shared the message of the birth, life, death and resurrection of our Lord and Savior Jesus Christ.

In his *New Believer's Growth Book*, Greg sets forth five things you need to do to become a part of God's family. If you've taken these steps, you can know without a doubt that you are a Christian. If you haven't yet taken these steps, I urge you to do so now:

1. Admit your spiritual need. Acknowledge to yourself and to God the truth set forth in Romans 3:23—you are a sinner.

2. Repent. Turn from your sin and, with God's help, start living in a way that pleases Him (1 John 1:9).
3. Believe that Jesus Christ died for you on the cross and rose again (Acts 16:30-31).
4. Receive, through prayer, Jesus Christ into your heart and life (John 3:16 and 14:13-14). Let the following be a model for you:

> *Dear Lord Jesus, I know I am a sinner.... I believe You died for my sins and then rose from the grave.... Right now, I turn from my sins and open the door of my heart and life. I receive You as my personal Lord and Savior. Thank You for saving me. Amen.*

5. Tell a believing friend and a pastor about your commitment to the Lord (Matthew 28:19-20).[4]

The New Testament gospel message is clear about what you need to do to enter God's family. And whether you just now received Jesus as your Lord and Savior or you did so decades ago, you are one of God's precious children. And short of blaspheming the Holy Spirit (Mark 3:29), you need not wonder about your place in His family. You're in for life—and for eternal life.

For new members of God's family...

> *Father God, I hardly know where to begin to thank You for what You have revealed to me about Your Son Jesus Christ. As You know, at this point I understand very little about who You are, but I'm willing to begin a new life with You at the center. Thank You for showing me the simple steps of*

———— ❖ ————

becoming a Christian. Now help me learn a little more about You each day. Surround me with godly friends and a strong pastor who can show me the way as, from this day forward, I trust my life to You. Amen.

For other members of God's family...

Father God, thank You for what You have revealed to me about Your Son Jesus Christ. You first helped me recognize Him as Lord and Savior, and since then You have continued to teach me more about Him. May I continue to grow in my knowledge of Jesus—and help me be bold in my witness so that I may point the way to those who don't yet know Jesus. Amen.

Taking Action

If you've just committed your life to Christ...

- Tell one or more people of your new commitment to Jesus Christ.

- If you have a Bible, write down today's date on the inside cover. Refer to it when Satan makes you wonder if you are saved and you need to reconfirm the decision you made today .

- If you don't have a Bible, jot this date down or circle it on the calendar until you do have a Bible. Then transfer this date to your Bible. Again, let it be a reminder of the important step of faith you have taken.

- Find a church where you can grow in your knowledge

—————— ❖ ——————

of Jesus— and attend the worship services there this weekend. You might even let the pastor know in advance of your recent decision for Christ and of your interest in his/her church.

- Begin asking God to give you good Christian friends who can encourage you in your faith and support any lifestyle changes you want to make now that you are a member of God's family.

If you've been in God's family...

- Share with someone who doesn't know the Lord what it means to be a member of His family.

- Reflect on how your life has been different since you named Jesus as your Lord and Savior— and spend time thanking God for those differences.

- Evaluate your Christian walk. What are you doing to continue to grow in your faith and become more Christlike? What steps would you like to take? What step will you take this week?

Reading On

Romans 6:23   Ephesians 2:8-9
Luke 18:13   Matthew 11:28

Fearfully and Wonderfully Made

Scripture Reading: Psalm 139:13-18

Key Verse: Psalm 139:14

I praise you because I am fearfully and wonderfully made; your works are wonderful, I know that full well.

—— ❖ ——

You're special. In all the world there's nobody like you.

Since the beginning of time there has never been another person like you.

Nobody has your smile, nobody has your eyes, your nose, your hair, your hands, your voice.

You're special. No one can be found who has your handwriting.

Nobody anywhere has your tastes for food, clothing, music or art.

No one sees things just as you do.

In all of time there's been no one who laughs like you, no one who cries like you, and what makes you cry or laugh will never produce identical laughter and tears from anybody else, ever.

You're the only one in all of creation who has your set of abilities.

33

Oh, there will always be somebody who is better at one of the things you're good at, but no one in the universe can reach the quality of your combination of talents, ideas, abilities and feelings. Like a room full of musical instruments, some may excel alone, but none can match the symphony sound when all are played together. You're a symphony.

Through all of eternity, no one will ever look, talk, walk, think or do like you.

You're special...you're rare. And in all rarity there is great value. Because of your great value you need not attempt to imitate others... you will accept—yes, celebrate your differences.

You're special and you're beginning to realize it's no accident that you're special.

You're beginning to see that God made you special for a purpose.

He must have a job for you that no one else can do as well as you.

Out of the billions of applicants, only one is qualified, only one has the right combination of what it takes.

That one is you, because...you're special.[5]

Someone in your life—your wife, your kids—may need to hear these words today. And maybe that someone is you. Do you, like the psalmist, fully realize that you are "fearfully and wonderfully made"? Do your children and your wife know that about themselves?

For a long time at our house, Emilie and I have reminded our kids and ourselves that we are special with a red plate that reads "You Are Special." We use it for breakfasts, lunches, dinners, birthdays, anniversaries, and various other special occasions. We've used it at home, in restaurants, at the park, and at the beach. Maybe that's a tradition you could start at your house. (Traditions aren't just women's work!)

You might also have every person at the meal tell the person being honored why that person is special to him or her. Give the special person a chance to share why he (or she) thinks he is special.

Our red plate has become a very valuable tradition in our family. We all need to be reminded every once in a while that we truly are special.

> *Father God, help me realize that I am Your handiwork, "fearfully and wonderfully made," and therefore very special in Your sight. You knew me before I was made. You sent Your Son to die on the cross for my sins. Thank You for this amazing love— and help me to share it at home and let my wife and children know how special they are to You and to me. Amen.*

Taking Action

- What are three things that make you special?

- Who are you, the unique individual God fashioned? What makes you smile and laugh? What irritates you? What idiosyncrasies do you have? What helps you wind down?

- Now thank God for making you who you are.

- Write a note to a friend telling him why he is special to you.

Reading On
Psalm 40:5   Psalm 119:73

There are two ways to live life. One is as though nothing is a miracle. The other is as though everything is a miracle.

— *Albert Einstein*

"I'm Too Busy Sawing"

Scripture Reading: Exodus 20:8-11

Key Verses: Exodus 20:9-10

> *Six days you shall labor and do all your work, but the seventh day is a Sabbath to the Lord your God. On it you shall not do any work.*

In *The Seven Habits of Highly Effective People*, author Steven R. Covey tells a story that reflects the need for rest, renewal, and reawakening in our lives.

> Suppose you come upon a man in the woods feverishly sawing down a tree.
>
> "You look exhausted!" you exclaim. "How long have you been at it?"
>
> "Over five hours," he replies, "and I'm beat. This is hard."
>
> "Maybe you could take a break for a few minutes and sharpen that saw. Then the work would go faster."
>
> "No time," the man says emphatically. "I'm too busy sawing."

To sharpen the saw means renewing ourselves in all four aspects of our natures:

Physical—exercise, nutrition, stress management;

Mental— reading, thinking, planning, writing;

Social/Emotional— service, empathy, security;

Spiritual— spiritual reading, study, and meditation.

To exercise in all these necessary dimensions, we must be proactive. No one can do it for us or make it urgent for us. We must do it for ourselves.[6]

Can you identify with that man in the woods? I can. I know how hard it is to stop sawing even though I know that taking a break will help me come back stronger. And you may be a lot like me. But I've learned to take some breaks— and you can, too.

In the "Taking Action" section, you'll find some ideas for what to do when you stop sawing— and some of them may sound so good that they'll help you put the saw down. When you do— when you take time to renew yourself— you'll be better equipped to handle the demands and stresses of life.

Like all of His commands, God's command to keep the Sabbath— to take time for rest— is for your own good. If you're tired and weary and maybe even fearful of what will happen if you put down the saw, if you're uptight, tense, and short-tempered, you are ready for renewal and reawakening. Take the risk and see what happens.

Father God, I'm often overwhelmed by all that needs to be done. It often feels that I just don't have time to stop sawing. Living a balanced life seems like

*an unreachable goal. Help me. Teach me modera-
tion. Show me balance. Amen.*

Taking Action

❖ Below you'll find a variety of suggestions for things you
can do to find refreshment. So take a risk. Stop sawing
and see what it's like to live a life that's more in balance.

Physical

• Get a professional massage or take a sauna or steam
bath.

• Exercise regularly by walking, jogging, playing rac-
quetball, swimming, etc.

• Read a book on nutrition and begin to change your
eating habits.

• Take a stress management class.

• Take a walk on the beach, by the lake, or along a
mountain trail.

• Plant a garden.

• Walk or run in the rain.

• Volunteer for the United Way, the Cancer Society,
or the Heart Association.

• Help a friend in need.

Mental

• Listen to good music.

• Read a good magazine or book.

- Find a spot for meditating and reflecting.
- Spend some time alone.
- Write a letter to an old friend.
- Write out some goals for the next three months.
- Enroll in a class at a local college.
- Think of possible changes in your life.
- List everything for which you are thankful.
- Learn to play an instrument.
- Memorize a favorite passage of Scripture.

Social/Emotional

- Have a good cry (yes, men can cry).
- Have breakfast or lunch with a friend.
- Spend a day doing anything you want.
- Spend a quiet weekend with your wife just to regroup. Choose someplace close. Avoid a long drive.
- Visit a friend.
- Make a new friend.
- Volunteer your time at a school, hospital, or church.
- Help a friend in need.

Spiritual

- Read the Psalms.
- Meditate on Scripture. Read a short passage and

think long and hard about it.

- Read a book by a Christian writer.

- Join a men's Bible study.

- Visit someone at the hospital or nursing home.

- Examine your motives (are you self-serving or serving others?).

- Listen to good inspirational music.

❖ Now add your own ideas to each of the four lists. Learn to take a break and take care of yourself. God Himself knows the importance of rest. He gave us the Sabbath and He calls us to be good stewards of the body, mind, and spirit He gave us. It's more than okay to take care of yourself—it's essential!

Reading On
Matthew 22:36-40   Exodus 20:2-18

Do not think that love, in order to be genuine, has to be extraordinary. What we need is to love without getting tired.... Be faithful in small things because it is in them that your strength lies.

— Mother Teresa

Meet Sergeant Major Pestretsov

Scripture Reading: Ephesians 5:15-21
Key Verse: Ephesians 5:21
Submit to one another out of reverence for Christ.

———— ❖ ————

You've probably never heard of Nicolai Pestretsov, but now you may never forget him. He was 36 years old, a sergeant major in the Russian army stationed in Angola. His wife had traveled the long distance from home to visit her husband when, on an August day, South African military units entered the country in quest of black nationalist guerrillas taking sanctuary there. When the South Africans encountered the Russian soldiers, four people were killed and the rest of the Russians fled—except for Sergeant Major Pestretsov.

The South African troops captured Pestretsov, and a military communique explained the situation: "Sgt. Major Nicolai Pestretsov refused to leave the body of his slain wife, who was killed in the assault on the village. He went to the body of his wife and would not leave it, although she was dead."

What a picture of commitment—and what a series of questions it raises. Robert Fulghum, the teller of the story, asks these questions:

42

Why didn't he run and save his own hide? What made him go back? Is it possible that he loved her? Is it possible that he wanted to hold her in his arms one last time? Is it possible that he needed to cry and grieve? Is it possible that he felt the stupidity of war? Is it possible that he felt the injustice of fate? Is it possible that he thought of children, born or unborn? Is it possible that he didn't care what became of him now? Is it possible? We don't know. Or at least we don't know for certain. But we can guess. His actions answer.[7]

What do your actions say about your commitment to your spouse? What do your attitudes and your words reveal about your commitment to her? Standing by the commitment you made before God and many witnesses when you said, "I do" is key to standing by your wife.

Picture again Sergeant Major Pestretsov kneeling by the side of his wife's lifeless body, not wanting to leave the woman to whom he'd pledged his life even when his very life was at stake. That is a high level of commitment, and we are to be as committed. In fact, we who are married are to be as committed to our spouse as Christ is committed to the church He died for. Furthermore, as Christians, our marriages are to be a witness to the world of Christ's love and grace. Clearly, marriage is not to be entered into casually.

In light of the importance God places on marriage, Emilie and I take very seriously the premarital counseling we do. We never, for instance, encourage two people to get married if one is a Christian and the other is not (2 Corinthians 6:14). A marriage needs to be rooted in each partner's commitment to love and serve the Lord, or else the union will be divided from the start as the two people look in different directions. In addition, only a Christian marriage will result in a Christian home, a home which glorifies God and acts as His witness to the world.

I can vividly remember the evening Emilie and I were sitting on the couch in her mother's living room. I took her face in my hands and said, "Emilie, I love you, but I can't ask you to marry me." She was stunned. She couldn't understand why two people who were in love couldn't get married.

As I looked into her eyes, she asked, "Why not?" I answered firmly but gently, "Because you are not a Christian." Very innocently she asked me, "How do I become a Christian?" From that moment she began to consider whether Jesus might actually be the Messiah her Jewish people had long waited for.

After several months of seeking answers, Emilie prayed one evening at her bedside, "Dear God, if You have a Son and if Your Son is Jesus our Messiah, please reveal Him to me!" She expected a voice to answer immediately, but God waited a few weeks to reveal Himself to her. Then, one Sunday morning, she responded to our pastor's challenge to accept Jesus Christ as her personal Savior, and that evening she was baptized.

My being obedient to God has meant being blessed with a rich and wonderful marriage that is rooted in His love and dedicated to Him. Furthermore, vowing before God to love Emilie through the good times and the bad has reinforced my commitment to Him when the times were indeed bad. Had my vows been to Emilie alone, I might have had an easier time walking away. But God's witness of our vows and the foundation He gives to Christian couples enables us to stand together whatever comes our way.

> *Father God, it's sometimes difficult to stand by*
> *the commitment I've made to my spouse. I want to*
> *do my own thing my own way. Help me to stay true*
> *to the vow I made before You and other witnesses.*
> *Amen.*

Taking Action

- Today in your journal write out a fresh, new commitment to God and your spouse.

- Think back to your wedding day and review the vows you spoke. What do they mean to you today?

- What do you think it means to, in marriage, "submit to one another" in all things (Ephesians 5:21)? List five things you can do to show submission to your wife. Act upon one of them today and the other four within the next month.

- Develop the habit of "reflexive giving"— of giving without being asked. Blessed are those who give automatically and lucky are those who are married to them!

Reading On
Ephesians 5:22-33   Ephesians 6:10-18

Five Qualities of
Healthy Couples

1.   Healthy couples have a clearly defined menu of expectations. When a family agrees on a menu of options for quality life and relationships, they'll enjoy a healthy, successful family.

2.   Healthy couples understand and practice meaningful communication. Within marital and family communication, it's important to remember that you're trying to move toward the deepest level of intimacy.

3.   Healthy couples are associated with a small, healthy support group. Meet regularly with three or four other couples who have the same commitment to God and their marriages that you have.

4.   Healthy couples are aware of unhealthy or offensive behavior stemming from their heritage. The Bible says that the sins of a father are visited on the children up to four generations. I must realize that what I'm doing to my wife and children today could be directly related to my great grandfather.

5.   Healthy couples have a vibrant relationship with Jesus Christ. When Jesus permeates our relationship as a family we experience a calm and quiet spirit—we also know that He is our source of life.

— *Gary Smalley*
in **Seven Promises of a Promise Keeper**

Knowing God's Love

Scripture Reading: 1 Corinthians 13:4-13

Key Verses: 1 Corinthians 13:4-7

> *Love is patient, love is kind. It does not envy, it does not boast, it is not proud. It is not rude, it is not self-seeking, it is not easily angered, it keeps no record of wrongs. Love does not delight in evil but rejoices with the truth. It always protects, always trusts, always hopes, always perseveres.*

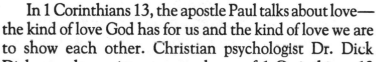

In 1 Corinthians 13, the apostle Paul talks about love—the kind of love God has for us and the kind of love we are to show each other. Christian psychologist Dr. Dick Dickerson has written a paraphrase of 1 Corinthians 13 which may help you hear God's message in a new way:

Because God loves me, He is slow to lose patience with me.

Because God loves me, He takes the circumstances of my life and uses them in a constructive way for my growth.

Because God loves me, He does not treat me as an object to be possessed and manipulated.

Because God loves me, He has no need to impress me with how great and powerful He is because He is God. Nor does He belittle me as

His child in order to show me how important He
is.

Because God loves me, He is for me. He
wants me to mature and develop in His love.

Because God loves me, He does not send
down His wrath on every little mistake I make,
of which there are many.

Because God loves me, He does not keep
score of all my sins and then beat me over the
head with them whenever He gets a chance.

Because God loves me, He is deeply grieved
when I do not walk in the ways that please Him
because He sees this as evidence that I don't trust
Him and love Him as I should.

Because God loves me, He rejoices when I
experience His power and strength and stand up
under the pressure of life for His name's sake.

Because God loves me, He keeps working
patiently with me even when I feel like giving up
and can't see why He doesn't give up with me
too.

Because God loves me, He keeps on trusting
me when at times I don't even trust myself.

Because God loves me, He never says there
is no hope for me, rather, He patiently works with
me, loves me and disciplines me in such a way
that it is hard for me to understand the depth of
His concern for me.

Because God loves me, He never forsakes me
even though many of my friends might.[8]

God loves us even though we're far from perfect. At
those times when we're very much aware of our failings, we

need to remember that we have value because we are God's. And knowing of God's love for us can empower us to love other people.

You've probably seen the bumper sticker—"Please be patient with me. God isn't finished with me yet." God is still working in our lives, and He'll never give up on us. As you become more confident of God's love for you, you'll find that people's opinions and judgments don't matter as much. Assured of God's unfailing love, you'll be able to serve Him and Him alone.

> *Father God, negative voices—from inside and out—can convince me I'm unlovable. But the Holy Spirit challenges me to believe that You love me. You even gave Your only Son, Jesus Christ, to die on the cross for my sins. I believe—help my unbelief! And then help me to confidently share Your love— in words and actions—with others. Amen.*

Taking Action

- What evidence do you have that God loves you? Make a list and then thank Him for these blessings.

- Review Dr. Dickerson's paraphrase of 1 Corinthians 13. Which phrases are most helpful? Why?

- Put your love into action. What can you do for your wife? At church? Can you help feed the homeless? Does the Salvation Army or a local mission need you for a few hours this weekend? What handyman projects could you do for an elderly neighbor?

Reading On

Matthew 5:46   1 John 4:12

The Call to Unity

Scripture Reading: Genesis 2:20b-25

Key Verse: Genesis 2:24

> *For this reason a man will leave his father and mother and be united to his wife, and they will become one flesh.*

One of Aesop's fables is the story of a wise father who, noticing disharmony among his sons, called them together to discuss the strife. He told each of his four sons to bring a twig to the meeting.

As the young men assembled, the father took each boy's twig and easily snapped it in half. Then he gathered four twigs, tied them together in a bundle, and asked each son to try to break the bundle. Each one tried but to no avail. The bundle would not snap.

After each son had tried valiantly to break the bundle, the father asked his boys what they had learned from the exercise. The oldest son spoke up: "If we are individuals, anyone can break us, but if we stick together, no one can harm us." The father said, "You are right. You must always stand together and be strong."

What is true for the four brothers is equally true for a husband and wife. If we don't stand together and let God make us one in spite of our differences, we will easily be defeated. That is one reason why, in this passage, God calls a husband and wife to:

- Departure ("A man will leave his father and mother...")

- Permanence ("And be united to his wife...")

- Oneness ("And they will become one flesh")

Together, these three elements help make a marriage strong. Let's first think about oneness.

In God's sight, we become one at the altar when we say our vows to one another and before Him. But, in reality, oneness is a process that happens over a period of time, over a lifetime together.

And becoming one with another person can be a very difficult process. It isn't easy to change from being independent and self-centered to sharing every aspect of your life and self with another person. The difficulty is often intensified when you're older and more set in your ways when you marry or, as was the case for Emilie and me, when you and your spouse come from very different family, religious, or financial backgrounds. Emilie, for instance, came from an alcoholic family and was raised by a verbally and physically abusive father. I came from a warm, loving family where yelling and screaming simply didn't happen. Although it took us only a few moments to say our vows and enter into oneness in God's eyes, we have spent more than 39 years blending our lives and building the oneness which we enjoy today.

Becoming one doesn't mean becoming the same, however. Oneness means sharing the same degree of commitment to the Lord and to the marriage, the same goals and dreams, and the same mission in life. Oneness is an internal conformity to one another, not an external conformity. It's not the Marines with their short haircuts, shiny shoes, straight backs, and characteristic walk. The oneness and internal conformity of a marriage relationship comes with the unselfish act of allowing God to shape us into the marriage partner He would have us be. Oneness results when two individuals reflect the same Christ. Such spiritual oneness produces tremendous strength and unity in a marriage and in the family.

For this oneness to happen, the two marriage partners must leave their families and let God make them one. We men help the cleaving happen when we show— not just tell—our wife that she is our most important priority after God. Likewise, our wife needs to let us know how important we are to her. We husbands can't be competing with our wife's father or any other male for the number-one position in her life. You and I must know that our wife respects, honors, and loves us if we are to act out our proper role as husband. And our clear communication of our love for our wife will strengthen the bond of marriage and encourage her love and respect for us.

Now consider words Paul writes to the church at Philippi: "Make my joy complete by being of the same mind, maintaining the same love, united in spirit, intent on one purpose" (Philippians 2:2 NASB). This verse has guided me as I've worked to unite my family in purpose, thought, and deed. After many years of working at it, I can say that we are truly united in our purpose and direction. If you were to ask Emilie to state our purpose and direction, her answer would match mine: Matthew 6:33— "Seek first his kingdom and his righteousness, and all these things will be given to you." As we face decisions, we ask ourselves, "Are we seeking God's kingdom and His righteousness? Will doing this help His kingdom come and help us experience His righteousness? Or are we seeking our own edification or our own satisfaction?" These questions guide both of us whenever we have to decide an issue, and that oneness of purpose helps make our marriage work.

Larry Crabb points out another important dimension to the oneness of a husband and wife when he writes this: "The goal of oneness can be almost frightening when we realize that God does not intend [only] that my wife and I find our personal needs met in marriage. He also wants our relationship to validate the claims of Christianity to a watching world as an example of the power of Christ's redeeming love to overcome the divisive effects of sin."[9]

God calls us to permanence and oneness in a marriage, qualities which the world neither values nor encourages. Knowing what God intends marriage to be and working to leave, cleave, and become one with our spouse will help us shine His light in a very dark world.

> *Father God, today's reading has helped me realize that there are several areas in my life where my wife and I need to be more united. Show me how to help work toward unity in purpose and spirit. I thank You now for what You are going to do in our marriage. Amen.*

Taking Action

❖ Set a date with your wife and, when you're together, write down five things you agree on regarding family, discipline, manners, values, church, home, etc.

❖ At the same time, list any issues which you don't yet agree on. State the differences and discuss them. Agree to pray about these differences. Then set a time for another date to again discuss these items.

❖ Say, "I love you" in a way you don't usually say it.
 — Fill a heart-shaped box with jelly beans, chocolates, or jewelry.
 — Give a certificate for a massage, a facial, or a weekend getaway.
 — Have firewood delivered—and then use it!

❖ We husbands show we care when we pay attention to small details.
 — Instead of handing her a pack of gum, unwrap a piece for her.
 — Pull out her chair as she sits down for a meal, whether you're at home or dining out.
 — Open the car door for her. Help her get in and out of the car.
 — Place a flower on her pillow.

Reading On

Philippians 2:2   Matthew 19:3-6
Matthew 6:33   1 Corinthians 6:19-20

Let us resolve: First, to attain the grace of silence; second, to deem all fault-finding that does no good a sin; third, to practice the grace and virtue and praise.

— *Harriet Beecher Stowe*

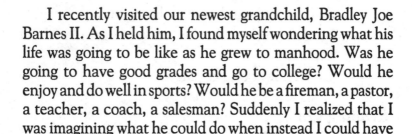

Finding Contentment

Scripture Reading: 1 Timothy 6:1-10

Key Verse: 1 Timothy 6:6

Godliness with contentment is great gain.

———— ❖ ————

I recently visited our newest grandchild, Bradley Joe Barnes II. As I held him, I found myself wondering what his life was going to be like as he grew to manhood. Was he going to have good grades and go to college? Would he enjoy and do well in sports? Would he be a fireman, a pastor, a teacher, a coach, a salesman? Suddenly I realized that I was imagining what he could do when instead I could have been praying about who he would be.

And maybe you find yourself focused on what you could be in the future rather than letting yourself be content in the present. I meet so many people who, unhappy in the present, are looking to the future— to the next paycheck, the next home, the next church, the next month, the next school, and, in some cases, the next marriage partner. (It's my thought that if you're not happy with what you have now, you'll never be satisfied with what you want.) These people live with the hope that the future will bring the missing piece to their life, the piece that means contentment.

Granted, it's not easy to be content. Our culture works hard to make us aware of all that we don't have. The advertising industry often makes us want things we might not otherwise have considered. We can easily find ourselves drawn away from spiritual pursuits and instead be building our lives around reaching a certain financial goal. Simply put, we find ourselves putting our hope in wealth (1 Timothy 6:17).

As I sat there in Bradley's room, I began praying for all of his extended family, that each of us would help teach him to value what God values more than money, career, and fame. It's not that these are evil, but placing too high a value on them can lead to our downfall (1 Timothy 6:9).

As you read in today's passage, Paul had learned that "godliness with contentment is great gain" (1 Timothy 6:6). When we find ourselves looking to the future because we aren't content with today, may God give us peace of mind and the ability to rest where He has placed us. May we pattern our lives after Christ and, walking in godliness, experience the rich blessing of contentment in the present.

Father God, You know that, like Paul, I want to be content in whatever circumstances I find myself, but You also know that too often I am discontent. Forgive me for valuing too highly those things which interfere with my pursuit of what You want for me and from me. You have given me so much and I thank You for those blessings. Teach me contentment, Lord. Amen.

Taking Action

- Instead of being preoccupied with the challenging or oppressive circumstances of your life, start praising God for where you are.

❖

- Ask God to reveal to you what you are to learn in your present situation.

- Write a letter to God and thank Him for the many ways He has blessed you. List those blessings individually.

Reading On

1 Timothy 6:11-21   Proverbs 22:1-2
Mark 10:17-25

Making and Keeping Promises to God

Scripture Reading: Romans 15:1-13

Key Verses: Romans 15:5-6

> *May the God who gives endurance and encouragement give you a spirit of unity among yourselves as you follow Christ Jesus, so that with one heart and mouth you may glorify the God and Father of our Lord Jesus Christ.*

---❖---

What if hundreds of thousands of men were reconciled to God and His will in every area of their lives? What if these men came together, united by their common love for Jesus? And what if these men then began to boldly take a stand for God in their families, in their churches, and in their communities? The possibilities generated by these questions are the hope of Promise Keepers, an organization that challenges men to dare to enter into the struggle for righteousness and, shoulder to shoulder, seize a divine opportunity to further the kingdom of God.

In 1990 a small group of 70 men in Boulder, Colorado, headed by Coach Bill McCartney and Dr. Dave Wardell, took the first step. They began to meet on a weekly basis and pray for each other. From this small beginning, the organization grew to 4,200 men in 1991 and 22,000 men in 1992. In 1993, 50,000 men filled the Colorado University football stadium for the express purpose of learning to take God at His Word. Then, in 1994, hundreds of thousands of men gathered in stadiums throughout America to hear anew God's call on their lives.

A Promise Keeper believes that we men will start making a difference for God in our world by first making some promises— promises we intend to keep. In fact, the organization has developed the following "Seven Promises of a Promise Keeper":

1. The Promise Keeper is committed to honoring Jesus Christ through worship, prayer, and obedience to God's Word in the power of the Holy Spirit.

2. A Promise Keeper is committed to pursuing vital relationships with a few other men, understanding that he needs brothers to help him keep his promises.

3. A Promise Keeper is committed to practicing spiritual, moral, ethical, and sexual purity.

4. A Promise Keeper is committed to building strong marriages and families through love, protection, and biblical values.

5. A Promise Keeper is committed to supporting the mission of the church by honoring and praying for his pastor and by actively giving his time and resources.

6. A Promise Keeper is committed to reaching beyond any racial and denominational barriers to demonstrate the power of biblical unity.

7. A Promise Keeper is committed to influencing his world, being obedient to the Great Commandment (Mark 12:30-31) and the Great Commission (Matthew 28:19-20).[10]

These promises are not intended to be a new list of commandments. They are not designed to remind us of how badly we're doing in respect to the often-competing demands of the marketplace, the home, and the mission field. Rather, these promises are meant to guide us toward the life of Christ so that He can transform us within so that, in turn, we might see transformation in our homes, among our friends, in our churches, and, ultimately, in our nation.

Why don't you become a Promise Keeper?

> *Father God, show me how I can find true purpose in my life— a purpose that gives meaning, excitement, and enthusiasm to daily living. I want more than what is offered by politics, sports, entertainment, and business. I want to learn what You originally designed me to be and I want to live according to Your plan. Direct me to a group of men who will be good role models and who will hold me accountable to my promises. Thank You, God, for placing within me the desire to be a man of God. Amen.*

Taking Action

❖ If you have not yet named Jesus as your Lord and Savior, seek out a godly man whom you respect and ask him to teach and disciple you. Find a strong Bible-believing church which clearly teaches the Word of God so that you can get to know God and His desires for His people.

❖ If you are a Christian and presently attending a church, go to your pastor and tell him of your desire to grow in your faith and to meet regularly with a group of other men. Find out what programs are available or what programs might be developed.

❖ Share with your wife and family your new or renewed desire to be a man of God. Ask them to support you in daily prayer and to hold you accountable to this new level of commitment.

❖ Someone has said, "I can't do anything about my ancestors, but I can do a lot about my descendants." What does this statement mean to you as you commit yourself to the Lord in a new way? What is God saying to you through this statement?

Reading On

Ephesians 5:14-16   John 10:7   1 John 4:7-12

Rejected by Men

Scripture Reading: Isaiah 53:3-12

Key Verse: Isaiah 53:3

He was despised and rejected by men, a man of sorrows and familiar with suffering.

———— ❖ ————

We've all experienced the pain of rejection, perhaps even rejection by someone we care about very deeply— a parent, wife, child, friend, brother, or sister, or possibly all of these people. Jesus Himself experienced rejection. If anyone knows the pain it causes, He does. His own people, whom He came to save, were the very ones who nailed him to the cross. As the gospel says, "he came to that which was his own, but his own did not receive him" (John 1:11).

My wife, Emilie, knows rejection from her people, too. Her Jewish family wanted her to marry within her own faith. Yet when she was 16, I introduced her to Christ. Within a few months we were engaged, and eight months later we were married. But Emilie's very own family rejected her because of her stand for Jesus and her decision to marry me, a Christian man.

God has honored Emilie's faithfulness to Him, and her family has come to respect and love me. The family has been restored, although it didn't happen overnight. In God's time, one by one, hearts were softened and attitudes changed. Emilie hung in there and loved her family when it was difficult because of their attitudes towards us and their mockery of our faith. She's grateful today that she trusted Jesus.

Emilie was rejected because she trusted the Savior whom Isaiah had prophesied would be despised and rejected of men. Jesus' foreknowledge, however, did not make the experience any less painful. But at least Emilie could turn to God in her pain. Jesus felt rejected by His own Father. As Jesus bore the sins of the world, He cried out "My God, my God, why have you forsaken me?" (Matthew 27:46).

Despite all this rejection, Jesus never abandoned the mission that God had assigned Him. He never fought back against the ones who rejected Him. Instead, Jesus responded with love— even for those who nailed Him to the cross.

When you are feeling rejected, remember that the Lord knows how you feel and that He offers you His strength. The Bible says that Jesus sympathizes with our weakness and offers His grace for our time of need. When Jesus suffered on the cross, He bore our penalty for us. He paid the price for our sins. Then He gave us a promise: "Never will I leave you; never will I forsake you" (Hebrews 13:5). No matter what happens, know that God will never reject you. You will never be alone again. You may be rejected by others, but remember God Almighty will always be there to comfort you.

Father God, You know how I needed this truth from Scripture today. You know the rejection I've experienced at work...in my family...with my finances. I lay before You all these hurts and ask for Your comfort and peace. I thank You for Your promises that You will always be near me. I need You today. Amen.

Taking Action

❖ What rejections— recent or distant— still cause you pain? List them.

❖ Rather than dwell on your pain, place it in Jesus' hands today with a prayer based on 1 Peter 5:7— "Lord, I cast my cares upon you, for I know you care for me."

❖ Despite the pain you're feeling, spend some time thanking God that He will never forsake you (Deuteronomy 4:31) and that, even if your mother, father, sister, and brother forsake you, He will take care of you (Psalm 27:10).

Reading On

John 1:2   Hebrews 4:15-16
Hebrews 13:5   2 Corinthians 1:3-7
            Philippians 4:13

If you feel far from God,
guess who moved?

The Minimum Daily Adult Requirement

Scripture Reading: Ephesians 2:4-9

Key Verses: Ephesians 2:8-9

> *For it is by grace you have been saved, through faith—*
> *and this not from yourselves, it is the gift of God—not*
> *by works, so that no one can boast.*

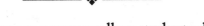

Several years ago a young college student asked me, "As a Christian, how much beer can I drink?" Others have asked:

- How long should I read my Bible each day?
- How long should I pray each day?
- How much money do I have to give to the church?
- Do I have to sing in the choir to be a good Christian?
- How many times a week must I be in church?
- Do I have to _____, _____, _____?

The list goes on and on. We all want to know what the minimum daily adult requirement is for being a Christian. What do we really have to do, day-by-day, to get by?

We're interested in daily nutritional requirements

when it comes to our food. Shouldn't we be as concerned when it comes to our Christian walk and our spiritual health? Of course! It only makes sense that we would want to know how long Christians should pray, how long we should read the Bible, how much money we should put in the offering plate, how many church activities we should participate in each week, etc., etc.!

Paul addresses these very basic concerns in his letter to the Ephesians. He very clearly states, "For it is by grace you have been saved, through faith— and this not from yourselves, it is the gift of God— not by works, so that no one can boast" (verses 8-9). Said differently, Christ has freed us from bondage to minimum daily adult requirements. Our relationship with the Lord Jesus is not contingent on works; it is a gift of grace.

"So," you ask, "do I do nothing as a Christian? Aren't there any requirements?" The Scriptures challenge us to be like Christ, and if we are to do that, we need to open the Bible and learn how Jesus lived. When we do so, we see that Jesus

- Studied God's Word

- Spent time with believers

- Prayed regularly

- Served those around Him who were in need

Christ did not do these things because He was told to do them. He did them because He wanted to do them. He did them out of love.

So what is your minimum daily adult requirement when it comes to your spiritual health? It will be determined by love. So let your loving God guide you as you go through your day and let your love for Him shape your Bible study, prayer time, giving, and other church involvement. Your walk will look different from everyone else's. That's okay when you're sure you're doing what God wants you to do.

> *Father God, help me not to worry about "how long" or "how often" as I try to live a life that pleases You. Put a strong desire in my soul to spend time with You today in prayer and study not so that I am doing what I "should," but because I love You and want to know You better. And in those quiet moments, let time stand still and help me forget about my schedule, commitments, and pressures as I worship You. Amen.*

Taking Action

❖ List the things you are doing because you "should," because you think they are required of you as a Christian. Cross off those items you are doing joylessly out of a sense of compulsion.

❖ Why are you still doing those things left on your list? Cross out any other items which you are doing because you "should" rather than because you love God.

❖ Now list only those activities you want to do because you love the Lord and want to be more like Christ. You may not change your list with this instruction, but now the items are listed because you want to do them rather than because you feel you should. Simply stated, you are learning to live out of grace, not the law.

Reading On

1 Corinthians 1:4-8   Ephesians 6:10

2 Timothy 1:9-10   James 4:6

2 Corinthians 12:9

A New Heart

Scripture Reading: Ezekiel 36:24-27

Key Verse: Ezekiel 36:26a
I will give you a new heart and put a new spirit in you.

As you spend time with God regularly, you'll realize that you, with your old heart, can't do what is necessary to make yourself a godly person. In fact, none of us can make that transformation happen under our own power—and fortunately we don't have to. In Ezekiel 36:26, God says, "I will give you a new heart and put a new spirit in you." God offers us a heart transplant, one that is even more remarkable than the transplants doctors can do today.

Thankfully, not each one of us will need a new physical heart, but each one of us does need a new spiritual heart. Why? Because we are born with a sinful nature. David acknowledges that fact in the psalms: "Behold, I was brought forth in iniquity, and in sin my mother conceived me" (51:5 NASB). The prophet Jeremiah writes: "The heart is deceitful above all things and beyond cure" (17:9). Jesus teaches that same lesson in the Gospels: "Out of the heart come evil thoughts, murders, adulteries, fornications, thefts, false witness, slanders" (Matthew 15:19 NASB). The apostle Paul wrestles with his sin nature: "For the good that I wish, I do not do; but I practice the very evil that I do not wish. But if I am doing the very thing I do not wish, I am no longer the one doing it, but sin which dwells in me" (Romans 7:19-20 NASB). And the apostle John is very direct in his statement about sin: "If we say that we have no sin, we are deceiving ourselves, and the truth is not in us" (1 John 1:8 NASB).

So what are we to do? Not even the most skilled physician can cure a sinful heart or give us a new and pure one. But God can and, according to His promise, will. In *Seeing Yourself Through God's Eyes*, June Hunt talks about this process:

> Slowly, after this divine transplant, healing begins and, as promised, your new heart becomes capable of perfect love. Your self-centeredness is now Christ-centeredness. There is healing to replace the hatred; there is a balm for the bitterness. You can face the world with a freedom and a future you have never known before.
>
> "Create in me a clean heart, O God, and renew a steadfast spirit within me" (Psalm 51:10). Once you have a changed heart, you have a changed life. You can love the unlovable, be kind to the unkind, and forgive the unforgivable. All this because you have a new heart— you have God's heart![11]

This kind of heart operation, at the loving hands of your divine Physician, doesn't require major medical insurance. There are no disclaimers or deductibles. God offers this transformation to us free of charge. It cost Him greatly— He gave His only Son for our salvation— but it's a gift to us. All we have to do is accept it— no strings attached.

Father God, You know that I need a new heart— not one that a doctor transplants but one touched, healed, and changed by You. I want that new heart with new desires, new direction, and new purpose, all of which honor and glorify You. I thank You in advance for all that You are going to do in my life. Amen.

Taking Action

❖ List five areas or situations in your life where you see the need for a new heart, for God's heart.

❖ Now, for each item you list, write down two or three activities you can do to try to be God's man in each situation. Know that God alone can change your heart but that you can make some choices to work with Him in the process.

❖ Choose a friend who will pray for you, encourage you, and hold you accountable in these areas.

Reading On

Psalm 51:5   Romans 7:19-20
Matthew 15:19   1 John 1:8
Romans 5:5

> Create in me a pure heart, O God, and renew a steadfast spirit within me.
>
> — *Psalm 51:10*

A Path of Purity

❖ *Decide to follow God's principles for how to live your life.*

You must make a conscious decision to choose God's ways. But then you can trust that He will stand by those who stand by Him.

❖ *Choose each day to serve God.*

Start each day by meeting God in prayer and Bible study. Doing so prepares you to listen for His guidance and walk through the day being mindful of Him.

❖ *Know your areas of weakness and avoid them.*

Don't let Satan hit you unexpectedly where you're vulnerable.

❖ *Don't try to serve two masters.*

You can't serve the gods of this world (money, success, prestige, etc.) and the God of the universe at the same time. In Matthew 6:21, Jesus warns that "where your treasure is, there will your heart be also."

❖ *Protect your thought life.*

God calls you to guard your mind as one of your prized possessions. That's one reason why, in Philippians 4:8, He commands you to think on good things. After all, your mind determines your actions.

❖ *Beware of what you see with your eyes.*

Don't be deceived by the visions of your eyes. As appealing as it can be, what the world offers leads to death.

❖ *Be careful about the little things of life.*

Little things have a way of becoming big things, so don't compromise your godly standards in the slightest. Stand strong in God whether the issue is big or...small.[12]

— Jerry Kirk
in **The Seven Promises of a Promise Keeper**

It Has an "Off" Button

Scripture Reading: 1 Corinthians 6:12-20

Key Verse: 1 Corinthians 6:12

"Everything is permissible for me"— but not everything is beneficial.

No greater influence impacts our thinking than the media. Unfortunately, our media in America is controlled by secular humanists, so the slant of most print copy, programming, advertising, and news portrays a secular life view.

Secular humanism is the view that man establishes his own moral values apart from the influence of anyone (including God), and he self-determines his destiny—he is the "master of his own fate."

The problem with such a life view is that it has no absolutes, everything is relative— it has no eternal reference point. We can make up our own rules as we go. But how do we know if sexual promiscuity is immoral or not? Why shouldn't we cheat in business? Why should family life be valued higher than career?

Ted Koppel, the news anchor for ABC's "Nightline," in a 1987 commencement address at Duke University said, "We have reconstructed the Tower of Babel and it is a television antenna, a thousand voices producing a daily parody of democracy in which everyone's opinion is afforded equal weight regardless of substance or merit. Indeed, it can even be argued that opinions of real weight tend to sink with barely a trace in television's ocean of banalities." This relativistic approach means we need to guard our minds more carefully, because so many kooky ideas are floating around.

Through the media and advertising, which relies heavily on subliminal suggestions, we are consciously and unconsciously lured to go for the Madison Avenue lifestyle. The secret of fanning our smoldering desires and wants has been elevated to a scientific approach. The economic goal of television is, after all, to sell products and services!

Our problem may be more what our unconscious minds are exposed to than our conscious minds. According to Wilson Bryan Key in his book, *Subliminal Seduction*:

> The conscious mind discriminates, decides, evaluates, resists or accepts. The unconscious, apparently, merely stores units of information, much of which influences attitudes or behavior at the conscious level in ways about which science knows virtually nothing. The vast communication industry realized long ago the resistance to advertising which develops at the conscious level. However, there is little, if any, resistance encountered at the unconscious level, to which marketing appeals are now directed.

You see, we can at least somewhat defend ourselves at the conscious level, but most of consumerism's appeals are directed to our unconscious mind.

Perhaps the only way to overcome this dilemma is to reevaluate our sources of entertainment and information.

Personally, I have virtually stopped watching television and I am trying to read more books. First Corinthians 6:12 offers us a credo worth adopting:

" 'Everything is permissible for me'—but not everything is beneficial. 'Everything is permissible for me'—but I will not be mastered by anything."

My concern for myself is that my unconscious mind will be mastered in an area in which I have no ability to resist. Our unconscious mind has no walls around it and no sentinel at the gate.

Watch television commercials one evening and ask yourself, "If these commercials are true, then who am I, and what am I?" The life portrayed on the tube loves pleasure, sensuality, doesn't deny itself anything, and has a right to whatever goal it sets. I believe you will come to the same conclusion I did.

Recently Oldsmobile introduced an all-new Cutlass: new body style, reduced size, front-wheel drive. But the car met with very sluggish sales performance. I have a theory which the general manager of a local dealership concurs with. Since the changes in the car are so radical, people are waiting to buy them until they understand "who" and "what" they are if they own one.

In other words, so much of our identity is tied to what kind of car we drive, an advertising campaign is needed to define who and what you are if you drive this new Cutlass. Since it is a well-built, stylish car, sales will surely take off like a rocket as soon as the car is positioned properly. That's the power of the media.

Remember the heroes you grew up with? Roy Rogers, Gene Autry, Sky King, John Wayne—men of adventure, honor, and justice. The prime-time heroes of our contemporary society are shaped by the creative penmanship of morally bankrupt humanists.

Frankly, I believe they represent a minority view. Many great examples of genuine accomplishment, faith, and courage abound, but they are supplanted by the neutered characters of the media owners.

Wouldn't we want the models for our children to be in the sacrifices and contributions of famous scientists, artist, thinkers, missionaries, statesmen, builders, and other heroes and saints? They are out there, but we are not going to find them through the media.[13]

Patrick Morley gives us a lot to think about in this excerpt from his book *The Man in the Mirror*. The insidious power of television is destroying our family life. As men, we have to take control of what we allow to come into our homes. We'd call the police if a burglar entered our homes and stole something of value—and that is what television is doing. As our key verse today teaches, what is permissible is not always beneficial. That is a warning to heed when we're considering the power of TV.

Think about the role the TV plays in your home. Are you or your family members addicted to television? Can you go a week without having the television on? Try it and see what happens. If nerves are on edge, tempers are flaring, and people are angry, these could be signs that you're too dependent on television for entertainment and escape. As the head of the family, take the lead in getting this stealer of time under control.

Father God, You know that I want the best for me and my family. I want to protect them from all that would hurt and rob them. Make me aware of those things which steal from us. Give me the courage to be strong in this and, if necessary, turn off the television in our home. Amen.

Taking Action

❖ Evaluate the amount of time you and/or your family watch television. What kinds of programs do you watch? If they are sending false messages about life, you may want to develop an alternate plan for using your time more efficiently.

❖ What could you and your family do instead of watching television? Here are some ideas: go to a play or a concert; have a picnic; watch family slides/movies; read books; listen to good music; talk together about life, the day-to-day and the big picture; take a walk; exercise; jog; swim; etc. Choose one to do this weekend and a second to do next weekend.

❖ What can you, as the head of the home, do to build up the family when so much of society is trying to tear it down? What activities can you plan?

Reading On
Ephesians 4:29   1 Corinthians 10:23-24

> Say no to good things, and save your yeses for the best.

"Come" and "Stop"

Scripture Reading: Genesis 22:8

Key Verse: Genesis 22:8

> *Abraham answered, "God himself will provide the lamb for the burnt offering, my son." And the two of them went on together.*

———— ❖ ————

"Come" and "stop." We were firm about teaching our children these words as they were growing up. These two words helped us raise our children because children who learn them learn obedience. And, as God's children, these are words we need to listen for Him to say and then we need to willingly obey.

Abraham is a striking example of obedience to God even when God puts Abraham to the ultimate test. God instructed Abraham to take his son Isaac to Moriah and sacrifice him as a burnt offering there. What must Abraham have thought? He deeply loved Isaac, the miracle child for whom he and his wife Sarah had prayed long and hard. And now God was asking him to sacrifice Isaac.

Early the next morning, Abraham, Isaac, and two servants got ready to go to the mountain in Moriah. Having cut enough wood for the burnt offering, they set out as God had instructed. "On the third day Abraham looked up and saw the place in the distance. He said to his servants, 'Stay here with the donkey while I and the boy go over there. We will worship and then *we* will come back to you' " (Genesis 22:5, emphasis added).

"We will worship. *We* will come back." Abraham, who had experienced the mighty power of God when he received the gift of his son late in his life, trusted God and kept moving ahead in obedience to God. I'm sure the servants were puzzled—as was Isaac. Where was the sacrifice? The servants didn't ask. Isaac didn't ask.

"Abraham took the wood for the burnt offering and placed it on his son Isaac, and he himself carried the fire and the knife" (verse 6). Perhaps in his early teens or maybe a little younger, Isaac was old enough to carry the heavy wood up a mountain.

As father and son walked up the mountain, they talked together. "Isaac spoke up and said to his father Abraham, 'Father?' 'Yes, my son?' Abraham replied. 'The fire and the wood are here,' Isaac said, 'but where is the lamb for the burnt offering?' " (verse 7). Where would they find a lamb in the wilderness?

Hear Abraham's reply: "God himself will provide the lamb for the burnt offering my son" (verse 8). So the two of them went on together until they reached the place God had told Abraham to go to. Once there, Abraham removed the wood from Isaac's back, built an altar for worship, and then arranged the wood on top.

Then he said to Isaac, "Come," placed his son on top of the wood, and bound him on the altar. Note that, like his father, Isaac was obedient. (He must have learned it from Abraham.) When Abraham said, "Come," Isaac went to his own father whom he loved and trusted and who loved and trusted his heavenly Father. At this point, Isaac must have realized with terror that he was the burnt offering, but the Bible doesn't reveal anything about Isaac's words or thoughts. Perhaps because of Abraham's trust and belief, Isaac knew too that God would provide. And maybe was willing to die for God. Whatever Isaac was thinking or feeling, there he was, bound and lying on top of the wood he himself had carried.

Now when an animal was sacrificed as an offering to God, it was bound—like Isaac—on an altar of wood, the knife was plunged into its throat, and the animal was sliced down the middle through its stomach. Clearly, everything was in place. It was time for the sacrifice. "[Abraham] reached out his hand and took the knife to slay his son" (verse 10).

Abraham's arm was lifted up, ready to plunge the knife into Isaac's throat, when "the angel of the Lord called out to him from heaven, 'Abraham! Abraham!' " (verse 11). Abraham *stopped.* "'Do not lay a hand on the boy,' he said. 'Do not do anything to him. Now I know that you fear God because you have not withheld from me your son, your only son.' Abraham looked up and there in the thicket he saw a ram caught by its horns. He went and took the ram and sacrificed it as a burnt offering instead of his son" (verses 12-13). That was a close call!

Abraham named that place on top of the mountain "The Lord Will Provide." Abraham had not doubted that God would provide. But can you imagine what the two servants must have thought when they saw both Abraham and Isaac return without any wood but with a bloodstained knife? Abraham had said, "*We* will return." They had worshiped God, and they had returned.

"Come" and "stop"— these are key words in the story of Abraham and Isaac. First, Isaac obeyed when his father said, "*Come* with me to worship" and then, "*Come* and get on the pile of wood." Abraham obeyed when God told him to prepare to sacrifice his son. And, when the angel called his name, Abraham stopped to listen. Had neither father or son obeyed, they would not have seen the Lord God provide for them so graciously. With their obedience came a greater knowledge of God and His mercy and love. "Come" and "stop" are two very important words when we, like Abraham and Isaac, walk with God.

How does your level of obedience compare with Abraham's? It's easy to say we trust God but then go ahead and take the situation into our own hands, trying to move ahead in our power and not allowing the Lord to provide the burnt offering. When we do so, we miss out on experiencing God's faithfulness.

What do you need to trust God for today? Where do you need Him to provide for you? God is calling you to come to His altar so that you can watch Him provide. So, despite the pressures of the day, stop and worship. During those quiet moments, tell God about your concerns and let Him remind you that He will provide.

> *Father God, may I come when I hear Your voice and stop when You call. Give me ears to hear Your voice and a heart to respond.... When I worship, teach me what You want me to know.... Remind me of Your faithfulness in the past as I try to trust You for the present and the future. Thank You that You will provide. Amen.*

Taking Action

❖ Choose a place in your home where you can worship—and then use it.

❖ Come and worship.

- ❖ Stop and listen.
- ❖ Trust God.
- ❖ Obey His Word.

Reading On

Galatians 4:28   Hebrews 11:17-19

The Owner's Manual

Scripture Reading: 1 Corinthians 16:1-24

Key Verses: 1 Corinthians 16:13-14

Be on your guard; stand firm in the faith; be men of courage; be strong. Do everything in love.

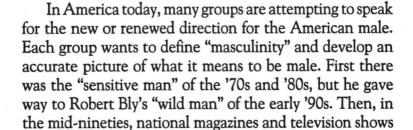

In America today, many groups are attempting to speak for the new or renewed direction for the American male. Each group wants to define "masculinity" and develop an accurate picture of what it means to be male. First there was the "sensitive man" of the '70s and '80s, but he gave way to Robert Bly's "wild man" of the early '90s. Then, in the mid-nineties, national magazines and television shows pronounced the men's movement dead and declared the "post-sensitive man" in vogue.

The heroes for this post-sensitive man, according to writer Harry Stein in *Esquire* magazine, are Rush Limbaugh, Howard Stern, and Jerry Seinfeld. According to Stein, these men have "trampled the corpse of Mr. Sensitive and given men the freedom to be guys again." [14] On the television program "Good Morning America," Stein further explained, "I believe we are reaching a period where men are allowed to be themselves again. Authentic behavior is back in vogue. People can say what they think without apology." [15]

It's not hard to understand why many men are confused

about who they are as men. We now have the post-sensitive man who is nothing more than a modern-day version of the '50s man, but is too young to remember the shortcomings of men in that decade. The bottom line? Men continue to search for their true identity in wrong places. The sensitive man, the wild man, the macho man, the feminized man, and even the post-sensitive man will ultimately be disappointed. So the discussion of real masculinity continues.

In *King, Warrior, Magician, Lover*, for instance, authors Robert Moore and Douglas Gillette write:

> It is our experience that deep within every man are blueprints, what we can also call 'hard wiring,' for the calm and positive mature masculine...instinctual patterns and energy configurations probably inherited genetically throughout the generations of our species. These archetypes provide the very foundations of our behaviors— our thinking, our feeling, and our characteristic human reactions. They are the image makers that artists and poets and religious prophets are close to.[16]

Robert Bly, author of the landmark book *Iron John*, points to what he calls "the old stories":

> The knowledge of how to build a nest in a bare tree, how to fly to the wintering place, how to perform the mating dance— all of this information is stored in the reservoirs of the bird's instinctual brain. But human beings, sensing how much flexibility they might need in meeting new

situations, decided to store this sort of knowledge outside the instinctual system; they stored it in stories. Stories, then— fairy stories, legends, myths, hearth stories— amount to a reservoir where we keep new ways of responding that we can adopt when the conventional and current ways run out.[17]

As interesting as Bly, Moore, and Gillette are, we have to go beyond folktales to the truth of the Bible in order to find out the real nature of men. We have to go beyond the spokesmen in today's culture to see how God intends us to live. The Bible— not what some writer, athlete, politician, philosopher, or actor might say about manhood—is the owner's manual for our masculinity.

And a growing number of men are opening the Bible and looking straight at Jesus to learn who they are as men. As a result, they are finding the fulfillment they haven't found elsewhere. More and more men are discovering what true Christianity is all about, liking what they find, and making a lifetime commitment to Christ. They are also discovering God's truth about masculinity and living lives characterized by courage, strength, and Christian love. With this new commitment and this biblical understanding of who they are as men, they are making a real difference in their families, churches, and communities.

In the end, only one type of man will be comfortable with who he is and truly fulfilled, and that man is a godly man. Read about him in the Bible and find there the one perfect role model. His name is Jesus Christ. Get to know Him better.

Father God, give me the insight I need to see through the mass media's definition of manhood. Enable me to discern what Your holy Word says about manhood. I want to know the truth—Your truth—about what it means to be a man. I want to know Jesus better and live more like Him. I want to be Your man. Amen.

Taking Action

❖ What are some of the media's false messages about manhood?

❖ Identify which of these messages are influencing your life and ask for God to show you His truth and help you live according to it.

❖ Discuss with a godly man those cultural influences you listed and learn how he combats the false messages.

❖ Study the Scriptures (the passages below and others) and learn what God says about manhood.

Reading On

Judges 6:16   2 Timothy 1:3-12
2 Samuel 22:31   Psalm 1
                Romans 8:1-4

> Father, I want to know the truth—Your truth—about what it means to be a man.

Guys Aren't Perfect

Guys are in trouble. Manhood, once an opportunity for achievement, now seems like a problem to be overcome. Plato, St. Francis, Leonardo da Vinci, Vince Lombardi—you don't find guys of that caliber today. What you find is terrible gender anxiety, guys trying to be Mr. Right, the man who can bake a cherry pie, go shoot skeet, come back, toss a salad, converse easily about intimate matters, cry if need be, laugh, hug, be vulnerable, perform passionately that night and the next day go off and lift them bales onto that barge and tote it. Being perfect is a terrible way to spend your life, and guys are not equipped for it anyway. It is like a bear riding a bicycle. He can be trained to do it for short periods, but he would rather be in the woods doing what bears do there.

— *Garrison Keillor*

A Five-Cent Cone

Scripture Reading: Proverbs 4:1-9
Key Verse: Proverbs 4:7 (NASB)
With all your acquiring, get understanding.

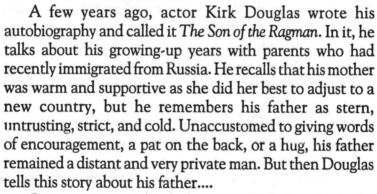

A few years ago, actor Kirk Douglas wrote his autobiography and called it *The Son of the Ragman*. In it, he talks about his growing-up years with parents who had recently immigrated from Russia. He recalls that his mother was warm and supportive as she did her best to adjust to a new country, but he remembers his father as stern, untrusting, strict, and cold. Unaccustomed to giving words of encouragement, a pat on the back, or a hug, his father remained a distant and very private man. But then Douglas tells this story about his father....

One evening at school, the young Kirk Douglas had a major role speaking, dancing, and singing in a play. He knew his mother would be there, but seriously doubted that his father would go. To his amazement and surprise, about halfway through the program, he caught view of his father standing in the back of the auditorium.

After completing the evening's program, he wanted his father to come up and congratulate him for a job well done, but true to fashion, his father wasn't able to say much. Instead, he asked his young son if he'd like to stop and get a five-cent ice cream cone. As Kirk Douglas reflects back

89

over all his awards in life, he prizes that five-cent ice cream cone even more than his Oscar.

As fathers, we don't always realize the important role we play in the life of our families. Our children hunger for our approval. They want and need to know beyond a shadow of doubt that we love them and care about what's going on in their life. Our kids need our words, but they also need our presence. They need us to spend time with them. And sometimes giving of our time says what our words can't or don't.

In today's key verse, God calls us to acquire understanding, and I challenge you to work on understanding your children better. Don't assume you already know what they're thinking and feeling. Let them tell you and then be ready to laugh when they laugh and cry when they cry. Be a dad they know really cares about the small and the big events in their lives.

> *Father God, today help me be an encourager for my children. You know how hard that is for me. Teach me to speak approving words and show them unconditional acceptance. Lord, I want to be a father who understands his kids. Help me start today. Amen.*

Taking Action

❖ Take your kids out for ice cream. Make this date with Dad a special occasion for them. Let each of them know they are special to you.

❖ Sometime today take aside each of your children, give them a hug, and tell them you truly love them.

Reading On
Proverbs 2:6-7   Proverbs 1:7

Not On Your
Permanent Record

Scripture Reading: Romans 8:1-9

Key Verses: Romans 8:1-2

> *There is now no condemnation for those who are in Christ Jesus, because through Christ Jesus the law of the Spirit of life set me free from the law of sin and death.*

An incident from the boyhood days of our son-in-law, Dr. Craig Merrihew, vividly illustrates the great promise in today's Scripture passage....

When Craig was in the fifth grade, he and a friend rode their bicycles to school each day. School started at 9:00 a.m., and they couldn't get on the playground before 8:30. One day the tailwinds were in their favor, and the boys arrived at the playground early. The fact that there was no supervision didn't stop them, and they were having a great time when a teacher finally arrived and sent the boys directly to the principal's office.

When they got to Mr. Fox's office, the two had to sit and wait, all the while wondering what was going to happen to them. Would they be expelled? Would the principal call the police? Would they go to jail? Would Mr. Fox call their parents to come get them? Their knees and their voices were shaking by the time Mr. Fox appeared and invited the boys into his office.

After hearing the story, Mr. Fox stood up and said authoritatively, "This will go on your permanent record"— the worst sentence Craig could have received. He just *knew* this would keep him from graduating from elementary school, junior high school, high school, and college, and definitely keep him from becoming a dentist. He also knew that his parents would be very upset.

When Craig got home that evening, he told his dad what had happened. His dad assured Craig that this event would not get in the way of any graduation ceremony or career plans—and those were words of freedom. Craig would not be condemned forever because of an early arrival on the school playground.

Have you ever been discouraged because you, like Craig, thought that some sin was on your permanent record? In Romans 8, Paul assures us that "there is now no condemnation for those who are in Christ Jesus, because through Christ Jesus the law of the Spirit of life set [us] free from the law of sin and death" (verses 1-2).

We are never to forget that, at one time, we were an object of God's holy and just wrath. But neither are we to forget that Christ Jesus came into the world to save sinners—and, like Paul, we are to feel that we are the worst of sinners. Aware of our sinfulness, we are then able to better appreciate the fact that Jesus died on the cross in our place. Jesus the sinless One bore our sins in His body and endured the wrath of God for us. When we see Calvary from this perspective, we see the love of God.

In fact, the love of God has no meaning apart from Calvary, and Calvary has no meaning apart from the holy and just wrath of God. Jesus did not die just to give us peace and a purpose in life; He died to save us from the wrath of

God. He died to reconcile us to a holy God from whom we were alienated because of our sin. He died to ransom us from the penalty of sin—everlasting destruction, shut out from the presence of the Lord. Jesus died so that we—the deserving objects of God's wrath—should become, by His grace, His children and heirs. Put simply, Jesus died so that our sins would not be on our permanent record.

And for assurance that your sins—past, present, and future—are forgiven because of Jesus' death on the cross, hear the words of John 1:9. These words are for you: "If we confess our sins, he is faithful and just and will forgive us our sins and purify us from all unrighteousness." Again, God's Word offers you total assurance that your sins will not be on your permanent record when you stand before God on Judgment Day.

> *Father God, thank You for giving Your Son for my sins...and for giving me the reassurance that all of my sins—past, present, and future—have been wiped from my permanent record because of His death and resurrection. I thank You for sending Jesus to be my Savior. Amen.*

Taking Action

❖ Spend some time in confession. Ask God to forgive you and purify you.

❖ Record this date and the reference "1 John 1:9" in your Bible so that you can look back and be reminded that God forgives us the sins we confess.

❖

Reading On

1 John 1:9   Luke 18:9-14
Matthew 5:1-10   Romans 5:14-21

Marriage Preservation

Scripture Reading: Proverbs 17:14-22
Key Verse: Proverbs 17:17
> *A friend loves at all times, and a brother is born for adversity.*

──────── ❖ ────────

Ed and Carol Nevenschwander (a pastor and his wife) write:

Although the shell of a union may endure, the spirit of the marriage may disintegrate in time unless mates take periodic and shared reprieves from the pressures they live under.

The pressures we must often escape are not those we create for ourselves, but those brought into our lives from the outside. Nonetheless, they can wear our relationships thin.

The key to keeping a cherished friendship alive may be found in breaking away long enough and frequently enough to keep ourselves fresh and our love growing. And usually that involves childless weekends. Without such moments of focused attention, it's difficult to keep the kind of updated knowledge of one another that keeps two hearts in close proximity alive and growing together. A growing marriage needs refreshed inhabitants.[18]

We live in a very hectic world that cries out for stillness, quietness, and aloneness. For the sake of our marriage and for our own mental health, we must seek out solitude. Such quiet times for regrouping don't just happen. You must plan to have these special times with your mate.

For the last 12 years Emilie and I have made it a point to get away from the noise and busyness of life and just be by ourselves. We don't set a schedule. We sleep in and disregard clocks; we eat when and if we want to. I encourage you to find a time when you and your wife can do the same. Our favorite time for these get-aways has been from December 27 to January 3. Whenever you go, be sure to get away from everything. Take time to write out some personal and family goals. With each goal, write out some specific action steps and a rough timetable for you. Slow down and rethink your life.

When was the last time you had any extended time alone with your wife? You may be thinking, "It's been a while, but we don't have the money!" Don't let excuses like this keep you from doing what you need to do to preserve your marriage. We have found that we human beings do what we want to do. You can find extra money somewhere if your marriage truly is a priority.

Father God, these words are convicting. I need to call a time out and work on preserving my marriage. Strengthen my commitment to my wife. Teach me to slow down to be alone with You...and to be alone with her. Amen.

Taking Action

❖ Plan a special day for you and your wife. Get away for

at least one night (two or three if you can).

❖ Set aside a fund for this adventure.

❖ Mail your wife a special letter of invitation.

❖ Keep your expectations for this time modest. Too many expectations lead to great disappointments. Take off the pressure. Just let the time with your wife happen.

❖ Aside from this special overnighter, what will you do to know your wife better? Express your appreciation? Communicate better? Listen better? Share more about what you're feeling? Romance her? Court her? What will you do to remind yourself to take time just to hold her? To be affectionate? Be specific on each count— and then get to work!

Reading On
1 Corinthians 13:3-8

> Giving and gratitude go together like humor and laughter, like having one's back rubbed and the sigh that follows, like a blowing wind and the murmur of wind chimes. Gratitude keeps alive the rhythm of grace given and grace grateful, a lively lilt that lightens a heavy world.
>
> — *Lewis B. Smedes*

Do Your Friends Help or Hurt Your Marriage?

❖ *Do your friends build you up?*
Be with people who are positive and affirming, not people who want to tear you down.

❖ *Do your friends bring out the best in you?*
Friends who are good for your marriage will encourage the positive, not the negative, in you and your spouse.

❖ *Do your friends respect your privacy?*
Some aspects of your marriage are private and should not be shared even with close friends.

❖ *Are your friends a blessing to your marriage?*
Spend time with couples who model godly and healthy values and who seem to share a kindred spirit with you and your wife. These friendships are precious and few, but a quality few will be all that you need.

❖ *Do your friends value your friendship?*
Invest in friendships which are mutual and cover those friendships with prayer. Pray for your friends' spiritual growth, knowing that they are praying for your spiritual growth.

Dealing with Rejection

Scripture Reading: John 3:16-21

Key Verse: John 3:16a

For God so loved the world that he gave his one and only Son.

—————— ❖ ——————

When have you experienced rejection? Did it come with that gal in high school, a marriage proposal, college entrance applications, missed promotions, a home loan you didn't qualify for? Now think about how you reacted to the rejection. Were you hurt? Angry? Both? Whom did you go to?

You and I can go to Jesus when we're rejected. He who was nailed to the cross knows about rejection. Isaiah had prophesied that Jesus would be despised and rejected by men (Isaiah 53:3). The people He came to save were the very ones who had Him nailed to that wooden instrument of death (John 1:10). Then, on the cross Jesus shouted to God in heaven, "My God, my God, why have you forsaken me?" (Matthew 27:46). Even His Father had let Jesus hang on the cross all alone.

Despite the rejection He encountered, Jesus...

- Never abandoned the mission that God had given to Him.

- Never retaliated against those who scorned Him.

- Responded in love.

And, according to the writer of Hebrews, Jesus can sympathize with our weakness and pain and give us His grace to help us when we're hurting. These promises are for you and me:

- "Never will I leave you; never will I forsake you" (Hebrews 13:5).

- "Praise be to God...who comforts us in all our troubles, so that we can comfort those in any trouble with the comfort we ourselves have received from God" (2 Corinthians 1:3-4).

- "Having believed, you were marked in him with a seal, the promised Holy Spirit" (Ephesians 1:13b).

Jesus is with us when we're rejected. He will comfort us, and His Spirit will give us peace.

So when we're rejected, we can choose to let bitterness, depression, anger, fear, doubt or loneliness to dominate our life. But these negative emotions can destroy us; they can give Satan a foothold in our life. Or, when we're rejected, we can go to God the Redeemer. He calls us to forgive, to love our enemies and pray for those who persecute us (Matthew 5:44-45), and these commands are for our good. They free us from the kind of bitterness that kills our spirit and blocks our relationship with God. And it's only when we adopt Christ's attitude of forgiveness that we can fully experience His healing.

Also, when we respond to rejection with God's love, others will notice. People will be drawn to Christ, God will be glorified, and you will experience freedom from the past and from the pain you felt. Forgiveness isn't easy, but it's what God calls us to do. It's what Jesus— who knows rejection— helps us do.

> *Jesus, You know what rejection feels like, and I do too. When those times come, may I turn to You.... And when I think about rejections in the past, help me to trust in Your steadfast love for me, Your perfect plan for my life, and Your power to redeem the bad in my life.... Help me to forgive where I need to forgive...and, when I am tempted to reject someone, may I instead extend Your love. Amen.*

Taking Action

❖ Make a list of the times you've experienced some kind of rejection. What has God taught you from those times? How has He used those times to develop your Christian character?

❖ If some of the events you listed still cause pain, talk to God about it. Ask Him what He would have you do, if anything. Be willing to take the step if He seems to be directing you to make a visit, pick up the phone, or write a letter.

❖ Turn to the Bible for assurances of God's unshakable and eternal love for you despite how someone may be treating you.

Reading On
Philippians 4:13

When Mamma Ain't Happy, Ain't Nobody Happy

Scripture Reading: Proverbs 24:1-34
Key Verses: Proverbs 24:3-4

> By wisdom a house is built, and through understanding
> it is established; through knowledge its rooms are filled
> with rare and beautiful treasures.

❖

When Emilie and I were shopping in the Marketplace
in Charleston, South Carolina, a booth displaying
handmade dolls caught our eyes. I noticed right away the
one whose apron had the words, "When Mamma ain't
happy, ain't nobody happy." I smiled to myself and showed
Emilie the doll. Smiling as well, she said, "So true! If Mom's
happy, the whole family is happy."

But you probably already knew that! As husbands, we
can help make the whole family happy if we make sure
Mamma is happy! If we spent time knowing our wives and
finding out what makes them tick—and ticked—we would
truly enrich our family's lives.

I'm not saying that we are responsible for another
person's happiness because we aren't. Each one of us is
responsible to find our own happiness. However, we

husbands can set the stage for our wives so that their happiness can flourish. And, when that happens, we husbands will receive riches and blessings in return. Women give their all to their families when they feel appreciated and when they know their husbands care about their thoughts, their feelings, and their daily world.

So think about it for a minute. How well do you know your wife? What are you doing to keep her happy—to meet her needs and to let her know you love and appreciate her? Are you spending the time with her she needs? Are you listening when she wants to talk? Start today to do these things, and you'll be enabling her to be a loving mother and wife—and when Mamma's happy, everybody's happy!

> *Father God, forgive me for taking for granted the blessing of my wife. Help me see where I've been insensitive and unappreciative. And help me, every day, to let her know how much I love her and how much I appreciate all she does for our family. I want her to realize that I see Christ reflected in her life. I truly want her to know that she is a blessing to me. Amen.*

Taking Action

❖ Surprise your wife with an impromptu date. Call her and say, "Get dressed up. I'm taking you somewhere special for dinner tonight." Choose a romantic setting—and be sure to line up a babysitter if you need one. Don't leave that to her.

❖ Leave your wife a small present—a single flower, a piece of her favorite candy, a small stuffed animal—somewhere in the house where she'll find it. Don't forget a card that tells her how much you appreciate her.

Reading On
Proverbs 9:1-6   Proverbs 16:1-4   Proverbs 4:5

In His Steps

Scripture Reading: 1 Peter 2:13-25

Key Verse: 1 Peter 2:21

> *To this you were called, because Christ suffered for you, leaving you an example, that you should follow in his steps.*

———— ❖ ————

Many years ago I read Charles M. Sheldon's book *In His Steps,* the story of a man who made a conscious effort to walk in the steps of Jesus. Before saying anything, doing anything, going anywhere, or making any decisions, he asked himself what Jesus would do and tried to do the same. Although living like Jesus was nearly impossible, this experience changed the man's life forever.

During our time on earth, daily situations will reveal our character—but will our character point others toward Jesus? We do well to look to Jesus and His example of a godly life. He showed us how to live with kindness, gentleness, sympathy, and affection. He was always loving, forgiving, merciful, and patient. He had a sense of justice and compassion for the suffering and persecuted, and He willingly took a stand for what was right in God's eyes. We can learn much from Him.

Jesus also tells us that He knows our pain, our grief, and the tragedy of friends who betray. He knows how hard it is to live in a world full of sickness and sin that we can do very little about. What we can do—and this is following in Jesus' footsteps—is bring people to Him, the One who forgives, heals, and helps. We can also let God work in our hearts and lives so that He can make us more Christlike—and that's certainly something the world needs today.

No, we can't be exactly like Jesus. Our humanness and sin get in the way. But we can develop a teachable spirit. We can love God with all our heart, soul, mind, and strength. We can let Him transform us into more selfless and more joyful people so that our character will reveal the likeness of Jesus.

As Jesus' representatives in the world today, we walk in His steps when we follow His call to us—when we help the helpless, pray for the sick, feed and clothe the homeless, and support those whom God lifts up to be missionaries where we can't go.

Let's try today to walk in Jesus' steps and respond to His call to serve.

> *Father God, You know I want to be more like Jesus, and I long for the wisdom only You can give. Grant me today some new revelation...and help me step out and trust You in a new way. May the time I spend reading and meditating on Your Word and praying help me know You better and may that awareness make me more able to walk in Your steps. Amen.*

Taking Action

❖ How teachable are you? What can you do to be more open to what God wants you to learn?

❖ ━━━━━ ❖ ━━━━━

❖ What will you do to follow in His steps today? Choose one or two items from your list and do them.

Reading On

    Ephesians 2:6-7   Colossians 1:15

Acceptable in God's Sanctuary

Scripture Reading: Psalm 15

Key Verses: Psalm 15:1-5

> *Lord, who may dwell in your sanctuary? Who may live on your holy hill? He whose walk is blameless and who does what is righteous, who speaks the truth from his heart and has no slander on his tongue, who does his neighbor no wrong and casts no slur on his fellow man, who despises a vile man but honors those who fear the Lord, who keeps his oath even when it hurts, who lends his money without usury and does not accept a bribe against the innocent. He who does these things will never be shaken.*

❖

Who can enter God's sanctuary? David answers that question in today's psalm by identifying 11 qualities of a person who is upright in deed, word, attitude, and finances. This righteous person:

1. Walks blamelessly
2. "Does what is righteous"
3. "Speaks the truth from his heart"
4. "Has no slander on his tongue"
5. "Does his neighbor no harm"

6. "Casts no slur on his fellowman"
7. Despises the evil man
8. "Honors those who fear the Lord"
9. "Keeps his oath even when it hurts"
10. "Lends his money without usury"
11. "Does not accept a bribe against the innocent"

These qualities don't come naturally to us. They are imparted by God through His Holy Spirit.

But being blessed by God with these honorable characteristics doesn't mean not struggling with sin—although it can look like that to us. You may look at a righteous person and think, "It must be easy for him to be a Christian. He apparently doesn't struggle with sin like I do!" But appearances can be deceiving. Living a righteous life comes when we choose each day to serve the Lord, and that's not easy for anyone. Living for God—living a righteous life—depends in deciding, moment by moment, to do what is right. When we do our best and when we rely on His grace, we will be welcomed into His sanctuary.

Father God, thank You that I don't have to rely on my own resources to live a righteous life. Thank You for Your Spirit that teaches and transforms me. And thank You for David's words today. Help me learn from what I've read and to live it out so that You might welcome me into Your sanctuary. Amen.

Taking Action

❖ What does it mean to you to be in God's sanctuary?

❖ Choose one of the 11 points in today's psalm and decide what you will do to improve that area of your life. List specific actions and take the first step today.

❖ What is your attitude toward worship? How regularly do you attend? Why does God call us to worship Him with His people?

Reading On

Psalm 27:5   Psalm 24:4   Joshua 24:14-15

For where your treasure is, there your heart will be also.

— *Matthew 6:21*

"Honey, Please Take Out the Trash"

Scripture Reading: Philippians 2:1-11

Key Verse: Philippians 2:3

> *Do nothing out of selfish ambition or vain conceit, but in humility consider others better than yourself.*

Not long ago Emilie and I had the good fortune to visit Canada and the town of Red Deer, a farming community on the flat plains of Alberta Province halfway between Calgary and Edmonton— a delightful spot any time but winter when strong Arctic winds make the area very cold.

After landing at the airport and clearing customs, we were met by Val Day, one of our hostesses for the weekend. As she drove us north to Red Deer, Val spoke modestly, but with the unmistakable pride of a mother and a wife, about her children and her husband Stockwell. She explained that her husband, who was in politics, would be home from the cabinet sessions in Edmonton over the weekend. That was the routine when the government was in session. Stockwell leaves home late Sunday afternoon, stays in his apartment in Edmonton through Thursday, drives back home to his Red Deer office Friday, spends the weekend with his family, and then starts all over again late Sunday afternoon.

I very much looked forward to meeting Stockwell B. Day, the Minister of Labor for Alberta Province. As the weekend neared, I heard all kinds of positive things about this very fine Christian politician. He was interviewed on TV during the six o'clock news, and the newspaper printed several statements made by the Honourable Day during this session.

On Friday evening we were invited to the Days' home for dinner. After Emilie and I arrived and introductions were made, we enjoyed a barbecue on the patio with the Day family and other guests. Emilie and I knew we were in the home of someone special—but for other reasons than you might expect. This man was tremendously respected by the people in his province, but what impressed us more was that his family was a high priority for him. This man of God is the head of a family that lives out love; they share a sense of humor, appreciation of one another, and mutual respect. It was a pleasure to share the evening with them.

After Emilie's seminar on Saturday, Stockwell and Val drove us back to the airport so we could leave early Sunday morning. During the drive, I asked Stockwell a question that I often ask successful Christian men. "Stockwell," I asked, "this week I've heard your name spoken with high admiration, I've seen the high regard your voters have for you, and I've heard you addressed by the title 'Honourable.' How do you stay humble and keep a proper perspective on who you are as a child of God?"

Without a moment's hesitation, Stockwell replied, "When I get home on Friday afternoon, I give Val a hug and then she very matter-of-factly says, 'Honey, please take out the trash.' With that simple request, I am back down to earth. I am reminded that I am a husband and father to a very special family before I am an Honourable Minister of Labor."

Men, that's what it's all about! We can have titles, fame, and wealth, but the Lord wants us, His children, to be humble in spirit.

> *Father God, thank You for making me who I am. I appreciate all that You have done for me and the many blessings You've given me. I want to stand before You humbly, recognizing that nothing the world has given me should make me arrogant or high minded. Please give me a humble and serving spirit in my family so that, as I empty the trash, change diapers, and help in the kitchen, I don't feel like less of a man. Amen.*

Taking Action

❖ How do you handle praise? Do you become self-righteous or are you able to remain humble?

❖ Do the people you work with consider you approachable? Why or why not? Is your humility or the lack of it a factor in how people feel about you?

❖ Do your children consider you a warm and approachable father? Why or why not? Is your humility or the lack of it a factor in their feelings about you?

❖ Does your wife feel that you are sensitive and receptive? Why or why not? Is your humility or the lack of it a factor in her opinion?

❖ In what areas of your life do you need to be more humble in spirit? Choose one of these areas to work on this week.

❖

Reading On

John 12:23-26	Job 42:1-6
Ephesians 5:21	Psalm 8

> Live by the Spirit, and you will not gratify the desires of the sinful nature.
>
> — *Galatians 5:16*

A Tough But Tender Warrior

Scripture Reading: 1 Thessalonians 2:1-16

Key Verses: 1 Thessalonians 2:7-8

> *We were gentle among you, like a mother caring for her little children. We loved you so much that we were delighted to share with you not only the gospel of God but our lives as well, because you had become so dear to us.*

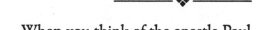

When you think of the apostle Paul, you may think of the Paul who endured imprisonments, flogging, stoning, and shipwrecks (see 2 Corinthians 11:23-27), and that toughness was very much a part of the fiery apostle. But today's reading reveals his tender side. He describes himself as being as gentle and tender as a loving mother is with her children. His hard-as-nails toughness did not mean he was without a tender side.

I saw such an example of a tough but tender man when Barbara Walters interviewed real-life hero "Stormin' Norman" Schwarzkopf, the four-star general who led the allied forces of Desert Storm to their Gulf War victory over Iraq. As this tough military man talked about the war, I saw tears in his eyes.

His interviewer noticed, too, and in her classic style,

Barbara Walters asked, "Why, General, aren't you afraid to cry?" General Schwarzkopf replied without hesitation, "No, Barbara. I'm afraid of a man who won't cry!" This truly great man knows that being tough doesn't mean being insensitive or unfeeling or afraid to cry. No wonder soldiers gave their best when they served under his command. They knew the general cared about them; they could trust the man giving their orders. We men want leaders whose hearts can be touched by our situations and who touch our hearts as well.

Even today, I vividly remember the encouragement that my high school and college basketball coaches would give me when they called me to the sidelines. As the coach explained the next play or the strategy for the game-winning maneuver, he would put his arm on my shoulder. That simple touch said, "Bob, I believe in you. You can make it happen."

Athletics can indeed be a real source of encouragement as boys travel the path to manhood. Granted, professional sports have become larger than life with the influx of the media dollars, but athletics remain a place where we can see the tender side of a tough athlete. That's what we're looking at when we see grown men jump into the arms of a coach or a teammate, two or more buddies high-fiving it, or a swarm of players jumping on top of the player who just made the big play. This childlike excitement is the tender side of the not-to-be-beaten athlete.

Are you able to give your friends a pat on the back or a bear hug? We're all on the same team— God's team— and we all need some encouragement as we head onto the field to make the big plays. We need each other if we're going to be victorious in this game called life.

Father God, thank You for reminding me that it's okay to be tender when I need so often to be tough...and for giving me Jesus as an example of toughness and tenderness.... I know that my family wants me to be more sensitive. They want me to take time to listen, to not be away from home so much, and to spend more time alone with them. And they'd probably even like me to be sensitive enough to cry.... I confess, Lord, that I am a husband and father who is often too occupied with myself and my job. Please help my family be patient with me even as You help me learn to be more tender with them. Amen.

Taking Action

❖ Plan and carry out a special evening with your wife. Romance her, not for your pleasures, but just to express to her your love for her.

❖ Spend some one-on-one time with each of your children. Go out for ice cream, play catch, or grab a Saturday breakfast. The plans don't need to be elaborate. The idea is to take time to get to know each one of them a little better.

❖ Ask each member of your support group what he does to express tenderness to his wife and children.

❖ Learn to give yourself away to your family (Ephesians 5:21). Watch for needs and work to meet them without being asked.

Reading On

2 Corinthians 11:23-27   Ephesians 5:21
Titus 2:6-8   Philippians 3:17-21

The Man God Wants

❖ Abraham *was faithful and believed in God (Hebrews 11:8-12, Genesis 15:6).*

❖ Barnabas *was a "Son of Encouragement" (Acts 4:36).*

❖ David *was "a man after [God's] own heart" (1 Samuel 13:14).*

❖ Hezekiah *"did what was right in the eyes of the Lord" (2 Kings 18:3).*

❖ Job *"was blameless and upright; he feared God and shunned evil" (Job 1:1).*

❖ Noah *"was a righteous man, blameless among the people of his time, and he walked with God" (Genesis 6:9).*

❖ Moses *"was a very humble man" (Numbers 12:3).*

❖ Demetrius *"is well spoken of by everyone—and even by the truth itself" (3 John 12).*

❖ Timothy *"is faithful in the Lord" (1 Corinthians 4:17).*

❖ Enoch *"walked with God" (Genesis 5:24).*

❖ Stephen *was "a man full of God's grace and power" (Acts 6:8).*

❖ Simeon *"was righteous and devout" (Luke 2:25).*

❖ Jesus *was "full of joy through the Holy Spirit" (Luke 10:21).*

❖ Cornelius, *the centurion, "and all his family were devout and God-fearing" (Acts 10:2).*

❖ Jonathan *"became one in spirit with David, and he loved him as himself" (1 Samuel 18:1).*

— H.B. London, Jr.
in Seven Promises of a Promise Keeper

Knowing What You Need to Know

Scripture Reading: Proverbs 1:1-7

Key Verse: Proverbs 1:7

The fear of the Lord is the beginning of knowledge, but fools despise wisdom and discipline.

———— ❖ ————

Most of what I really need to know about how to live, and what to do, and how to be, I learned in kindergarten. Wisdom was not at the top of the graduate school mountain but there in the sandbox at nursery school.

These are the things I learned: Share everything. Play fair. Don't hit people. Put things back where you found them. Clean up your own mess. Don't take things that aren't yours. Say you're sorry when you hurt someone. Wash your hands before you eat. Flush. Warm cookies and cold milk are good for you. Live a balanced life. Learn some and think some and draw and paint and sing and dance and play and work some everyday.

Take a nap every afternoon. When you go out into the world, watch for traffic, hold hands, and stick together. Be aware of wonder.

Remember the little seed in the plastic cup. The roots go down and the plant goes up and nobody really knows how or why, but we are all like that.

Goldfish and hamsters and white mice and even the little seed in the plastic cup—they all die. So do we.

And then, remember the book about Dick and Jane and the first word you learned, the biggest word of all: LOOK. Everything you need to know is in there somewhere. The Golden Rule and love and basic sanitation. Ecology and politics and sane living.

Think of what a better world it would be if we all—the whole world—had cookies and milk about 3 o'clock every afternoon and then lay down with our blankets for a nap. Or if we had a basic policy in our nation and other nations to always put things back where we found them and cleaned up our own messes. And it is still true, no matter how old you are, when you go out into the world it is best to hold hands and stick together.[19]

Robert Fulghum has a point when he says—to quote the title of his popular book—"all I really need to know I learned in kindergarten." As true as it is that we gain fundamental lessons for life in kindergarten, King Solomon wisely tells us that "the fear of the Lord is the beginning of knowledge," the kind of knowledge we need for life now and life eternal. In the Book of Proverbs, Solomon offers advice on how to conduct ourselves in various situations in everyday life. His basic instruction is to fear and trust the Lord, and he challenges us to continually seek God's wisdom for the decisions we must make each day.

The kind of knowledge Solomon writes about goes beyond academic accomplishments to moral responsibility. It focuses on decision-making and shows itself best in our self-discipline and moral living. It's far too easy, though, to raise our children to be lawyers, doctors, teachers, salespeople, or musicians, rather than teaching them, first and foremost, to be good, moral, godly people. Our society and the world in general desperately need good people.

Robert Fulghum shared his ideas, but we need God's ideas, too. We need to base our idea of right and wrong on an accurate understanding of Scripture and a solid knowledge of God's commands to us. We aren't to be swayed by what the secular world says. His Word tells us not to be conformed to the world, but to "be transformed by the renewing of our minds" (Romans 12:2). We must continually seek God's wisdom if we are to know His will for us, "His good, pleasing and perfect will" (Romans 12:2).

Father God, I want to be a man who seeks after Your knowledge. Show me Your ways that I might acknowledge You as God with how I live, what I choose, the words I speak, and the thoughts I think. Help me to see that You are all I will ever need. Amen.

Taking Action

❖ What decisions do you need to make today? On what basis will you make them— the world's teachings or God's Word?

❖ What can you do to get into the habit of looking to Scripture for guidance in your decisions and for answers to questions that come up?

❖ Do you have a verse of Scripture that serves as your theme for life? If not, ask God to give you one as you spend time in His Word this week. (I use Matthew 6:33 as mine.)

Reading On
Romans 12:1-2   James 3:13-18   Proverbs 3:1-18

Wisdom:
Learn What the Bible Says

❖ King Solomon was the wisest man who ever lived. Read 1 Kings 3:3-28. Here Solomon asks for wisdom and God responds. What does this teach you about the nature and the value of wisdom?

❖ The Book of Proverbs is a collection of wise sayings, most of which are attributed to King Solomon. Read Proverbs 1:1-7. What is the purpose of this book of wisdom? According to Proverbs 1:7 and James 1:5, how do we begin to acquire wisdom?

❖ The Book of Proverbs repeatedly reminds us that God wants us to acquire wisdom. Look at Proverbs 16, especially verses 1-3, 9, 16, and 21-23. What guidelines do you find for wise living?

❖ James 3:13-18 describes two types of wisdom. Which type is evident in your own life? How do you know?

❖ The Book of Proverbs has 31 chapters. Read one chapter each day and reflect on its teachings.

Have I Ever Seen a Christian?

Scripture Reading: Psalm 78:1-7

Key Verse: Psalm 78:4

> *We will not hide [God's commandments] from their children; we will tell the next generation the praiseworthy deeds of the Lord, his power, and the wonders he has done.*

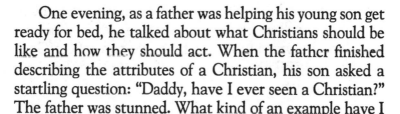

One evening, as a father was helping his young son get ready for bed, he talked about what Christians should be like and how they should act. When the father finished describing the attributes of a Christian, his son asked a startling question: "Daddy, have I ever seen a Christian?" The father was stunned. What kind of an example have I been? he wondered.

Imagine being asked that question by your son or daughter. Today's Scripture calls us to teach our children about God so clearly that they have no reason to wonder if they've ever seen a believer. The writer of Psalm 78 calls us to help our children know the things of God by telling them the many reasons we have to praise the Lord (verse 4) and teaching them His laws and statutes (verse 5). And such teaching happens as much— if not more— through our lives as through our words! Our children will look to us in the day-to-day situations of life to see what being a Christian looks like. That is one reason why God, speaking through Moses, instructs to "impress" upon our children God's commandments by talking "about them when you sit at home and when you walk along the road, when you lie down and when you get up" (see Deuteronomy 6:6-7).

It's a big order to fill. We fathers are to reflect God and His character to our children. As they look into our faces, listen to our words, and watch our lives, they are to see a man of godly speech, actions, and goals. Granted, you and I are in process. Our Christian growth comes day by day as, with God's help, we take off the old self—those attitudes, beliefs, and behaviors which reflect the dark, sinful side of our nature—and are transformed by His Spirit into a more Christlike person. Our children are watching this process. How are we doing? What are they seeing?

God calls us fathers to train and nurture our children in His ways, and that kind of teaching comes by our living example as well as by specific teaching times. When we ourselves are growing in our faith, we can reflect God's grace to our children, and they will know that they have seen a Christian.

Lord God, I thank You for the godly men You have put in my life who have modeled for me what being a follower of Christ is all about. They have been a real inspiration to my Christian growth. Help me to continually seek out such godly men who will live the Christian walk in front of me.... And, Lord, help me be that kind of person in my own home. Be at work in my heart and mind to transform me so that I can better reflect You for my children in all I say and do. Amen.

Taking Action

❖ Ask your children today what they think a Christian is. Learn from their response where you can sharpen your example. Make that area of your life a topic of your prayers and a focus of your efforts.

❖ Make thanksgiving the theme of a special time of prayer with your children. Let them hear you thank God for the blessings He has given you—and listen carefully to what they are thankful for.

❖ Consider the decisions before you today. Where do you have an opportunity to do something of eternal significance? Do it!

Reading On

Ephesians 6:4   Deuteronomy 6:6-7
           Ephesians 4:22-24

The LORD is close to the brokenhearted and saves those who are crushed in spirit.

— Psalm 34:18

What Mark Are
You Leaving?

If you're a dad, what kind of mark are you leaving on your children, especially your sons? Do you realize that your little boys are watching you like hawks? They're trying to figure out what maleness is all about, and you're their model. I hope they see in you a deep, uncompromising love for God. I hope they see both toughness and tenderness. If they do, then you have served them well; they will be forever grateful. Your little girls, too, will benefit because they'll grow up with a clear vision of the kind of men who make godly husbands.

— *Bill Hybels*

A Friend Who Prays

Scripture Reading: Colossians 1:9-12

Key Verse: Colossians 1:9

Since the day we heard about you, we have not stopped praying for you and asking God to fill you with the knowledge of his will through all spiritual wisdom and understanding.

———— ❖ ————

Have you discovered that geographic distance and passing years are ineffective obstacles for you and your real friends? It's true for me. Perhaps it's our common walk with the Lord that enables us to just pick up where we left off whenever we are together. Like the hidden but essential infrastructure of a building, these kinds of friends hold us up when challenges and trials come our way.

For me, prayer is an important part of friendship that lasts, and our passage today offers us an eloquent model of a Christian's prayer for his friends. Even though Paul had never visited the church of Colossae, his love for the people there was strong and ardent. As you read again today's Scripture, notice what a wonderful prayer it is for you to pray for your friends and for your friends to pray for you. Knowing that a friend is praying for me like this is a real source of encouragement and support. So if you aren't praying for your friends daily, let me suggest that Colossians 1:9-12 be your model. You'll be asking God to:

- Give your friend the spiritual wisdom and understanding he needs to know God's will.

- Help him "walk in a manner worthy of the Lord, [and] please him in all respects" (verse 10 NASB).

- Enable him to please God by "bearing fruit in all good work and increasing in the knowledge of God" (verse 10 NASB).

- Grant him strength and power "for the attaining of all steadfastness and patience" (verse 11 NASB).

You could then end your prayer by thanking God for all that He has given you, your friendship being one of those blessings (verse 12).

Now to which of your friends will you give the gift of this prayer? Tell your friend that you are praying for him each day and let him know the specifics of your prayers. With the Lord at his side and these powerful words being prayed for him, your friend will be able to boldly face the challenges of life and grow to become more the man God desires him to be. Let me assure you that it is a real comfort to have a friend praying for me like this, to know that he is asking God to enable me to honor Him in all I do, help me bear fruit for His kingdom, give me wisdom and understanding, and grant me strength, steadfastness, and patience.

By the way, these verses from Colossians are a good model for your prayers for your wife, other members of your family, your neighbors, and yourself. After all, every one of us who is God's child needs to know His will, honor Him in all we do, grow in our knowledge of the Lord, and be strong, steadfast, and patient as we serve Him.

Father God, thank You for blessing me with good friends. Thank You for this group of men who have helped shape my life. Without You and them, I wouldn't be who I am today. Help me to be faithful in my prayers for them, their families, and their walk with You. Amen.

Taking Action

❖ Write down the names of one or two friends for whom you want to pray each day. Under their names, list several specific areas of concern.

❖ Read Colossians 1:9-12 for 30 straight days. As you do so, pray for the friend(s) you listed.

Reading On

Ephesians 3:14-19   Philemon 1:4-7

> Trust in the LORD with all your heart and lean not on your own understanding; in all your ways acknowledge him, and he will make your paths straight.
>
> — *Proverbs 3:5-6*

Three Loves

Scripture Reading: Deuteronomy 6:4-9

Key Verse: Deuteronomy 6:5

Love the Lord your God with all your heart and with all your soul and with all your strength.

———— ❖ ————

Today's Scripture talks about three basic loves—love of God, love of neighbor, and love of self. And what a difference we Christians would make in the world if we were able to love this way. The passage goes on and challenges us to:

- Put these commandments in our hearts.

- Impress them on our children.

- Talk about them continually.

- "Tie them as symbols" on our bodies.

- Write them on our doorframes and gates.

Clearly, this command to love is important to God.

But, as we try to remain constantly aware of God's command, *how do we live out these three loves?* In his letter to the Ephesian church, Paul helps us start to answer that question by saying, "Be filled with the Spirit" (Ephesians 5:18).

❖

If we are loving ourselves, we will speak and sing words of joy. Paul commands us to do just that when he writes, "Speak to one another with psalms, hymns and spiritual songs. Sing and make music in your heart to the Lord" (Ephesians 5:19). People able to love themselves, people comfortable with whom God made them to be, will have lives characterized by joy, praise, and enthusiasm. Are you able to reflect the joy of the Lord? That's one way to tell if you're able to love yourself.

If we are loving God, we will be able to fulfill the command of Ephesians 5:20 by "always giving thanks for all things in the name of our Lord Jesus Christ to God, even the Father" (NASB). If we love God, we will find reasons everywhere for giving Him our thanks.

If we are loving other people, we will be able to "be subject to one another in the fear of Christ" (Ephesians 5:21 NASB). We will be less selfish and therefore able to willingly set aside some of our needs in our relationships. We will let another person's needs take precedence over our own. This kind of submission (and that word has certainly taken a beating in our society) is to be based on reverence for God. As members of God's family, we submit to one another out of respect for God.

Together, the commands to love God with all our heart, all our soul, and all our strength and to love God, others, and ourselves are a call to put first things first. And it's a daily challenge to do so.

> *Father God, You know the demands on me as husband, father, and breadwinner. Help me to meet those challenges by starting each day with the question, "What can I do to love God with all my heart, soul, and strength?" Help my relationships*

with others fall into place as I make loving You and loving them my goal. And help me better understand what kind of love You want me to have for myself. Your call to love seems so basic, but I know I'll be working at it my whole life. Amen.

Taking Action

❖ Write down several ways you presently live out your love of:

— God

— Others

— Self

❖ Now write down several new ways to love God, others, and yourself. Choose one in each category to start doing this week.

— God

— Others

— Self

Reading On
Ephesians 5:18-21   Matthew 22:36-40

The Temptation of Power

What makes the temptation of power so seemingly irresistible? Maybe it is that power offers an easy substitute for the hard task of love. It seems easier to be God than to love God, easier to control people than to love people, easier to own life than to love life....

The long painful history of the church is the history of people ever and again tempted to choose power over love, control over the cross, being a leader over being led. Those who resisted this temptation to the end and thereby give us hope are the true saints.

— *Henri Nouwen*

□ □ □

Harmony in the Home

Scripture Reading: Ephesians 3:14-21

Key Verses: Ephesians 3:17-19

> *I pray that you, being rooted and established in love, may have power, together with all the saints, to grasp how wide and long and high and deep is the love of Christ, and to know this love that surpasses knowledge— that you may be filled to the measure of all the fullness of God.*

———— ❖ ————

A traveler in Germany saw an unusual sight in the tavern where he stopped for dinner. After the meal, the landlord put a great dish of soup on the floor and gave a loud whistle. Into the room came a big dog, a large cat, an old raven, and a very large rat with a bell about its neck. All four went to the dish and, without disturbing each other, ate together. After they had eaten, the dog, the cat, and the rat lay before the fire, while the raven hopped around the room. These animals had been well trained by the landlord. Not one of them tried to hurt any of the others. The traveler's comment was, if a dog, a rat, a cat, and a bird can learn to live happily together, little children—even brothers and sisters— ought to be able to do the same.

Sadly, however, families are too often characterized by disharmony. When that's the case, we do well to model our

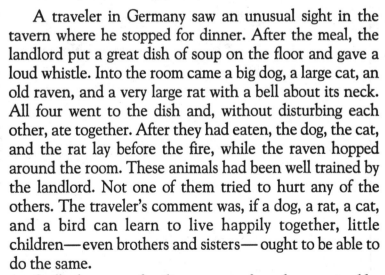

□ □ □

Harmony in the Home

Scripture Reading: Ephesians 3:14-21

Key Verses: Ephesians 3:17-19

> *I pray that you, being rooted and established in love, may have power, together with all the saints, to grasp how wide and long and high and deep is the love of Christ, and to know this love that surpasses knowledge— that you may be filled to the measure of all the fullness of God.*

———— ❖ ————

A traveler in Germany saw an unusual sight in the tavern where he stopped for dinner. After the meal, the landlord put a great dish of soup on the floor and gave a loud whistle. Into the room came a big dog, a large cat, an old raven, and a very large rat with a bell about its neck. All four went to the dish and, without disturbing each other, ate together. After they had eaten, the dog, the cat, and the rat lay before the fire, while the raven hopped around the room. These animals had been well trained by the landlord. Not one of them tried to hurt any of the others. The traveler's comment was, if a dog, a rat, a cat, and a bird can learn to live happily together, little children—even brothers and sisters— ought to be able to do the same.

Sadly, however, families are too often characterized by disharmony. When that's the case, we do well to model our

136

prayers for our family after Paul's words in today's reading. The things he prays for can lead to harmony at home.

- Pray that your family may be "rooted and established in love" (verse 17). God's love can help us be patient and kind with one another. God's love is not envious, boastful, or proud. His love is not rude, self-seeking, or easily angered, and it does not keep track of wrongs. Furthermore, it protects, trusts, hopes, and perseveres (see 1 Corinthians 13:4-7). Isn't this the kind of love you want in your family? Then ask God to fill your home and your hearts with His love.

- Pray that each member of your family would be able "to grasp how wide and long and high and deep is the love of Christ" for him or her (verse 18). Knowing Christ's immeasurable love for us, knowing that He loves us just as we are, knowing that He made us special and unique, and knowing that He died for our sins enables us to love one another. May the members of your family begin to grasp the vastness of Christ's love for them, individually and collectively, so that they can more freely love each other.

- Pray that each family member would "know this love that surpasses knowledge" (verse 19). Because of our human limitations, such as they are, we cannot fully comprehend God's love for us, a love that let Jesus die for us. God's love is beyond our knowledge of human love. But accepting in faith this gracious love helps us live out the gospel in our life and in our family.

- Pray that each member of your family will "be filled to the measure of all the fullness of God" (verse 19).

Each day I read God's Word, I learn more about His patience, mercy, forgiveness, joy, justice, kindness, compassion— the list goes on and on. Can you imagine being filled completely full with these characteristics of God? Can you imagine each member of your family being filled with these qualities? What a wonderful place your home would be! And that is what this prayer is all about!

I can't imagine a more relevant prayer for your family than these lines by the apostle Paul. Make Paul's prayer for the believers in Ephesus your prayer for yourself and your family and then watch God work to bring harmony to your home.

> *Father God, You know the tensions in our family and You know where we fail to love each other. I earnestly pray that You would work in our hearts to root and establish us in Your love. Help each one of us realize how wide, how long, how high, and how deep Your love for us is. I pray this for myself and I pray this for my family, that we may glorify You in our home. Amen.*

Taking Action

❖ Make a point of telling each member of your family today that you love him/her.

❖ Then do something to show a member of your family that you love him/her.

❖ Hugs are therapeutic. Your family members will be better at expressing love if they receive at least one hug a day. Get to work!

Reading On

Ephesians 4:29   Proverbs 24:3-4
James 1:22-23   James 2:15-17

> Don't let what you cannot do interfere with
> what you can do.
>
> — *John Wooden*

We Belong in Families

No matter how difficult life becomes, we belong in families. There may be times when we let down those we love and fail people who care the most, but through it all we discover a group of people who make us feel that we belong, who say, "What happens to you matters to me." Thus we stand together and face all of life with a confidence born of a sure identity in the family....

In spite of the pain, frustration and embarrassment, the unavoidable world of life in the family is still God's gift. The caring, nurture and confidence that comes from being seen at our worst and still knowing that we belong is his gift to us. It is the place where we can...love one another over the long haul. It is a place where we see his power and grace demonstrated over and over again.

— *John F. Westfall*

Living with Joy

Scripture Reading: Psalm 40:1-4

Key Verse: Psalm 40:3

He put a new song in my mouth, a hymn of praise to our God.

———— ❖ ————

What would life be like without joy? Without joy, we would be like a violin out of tune, yielding only harsh sounds. Without joy, life would be like a bone out of joint, unable to function properly. We can do nothing well without joy.

And God is the only source of real joy. When we come before God with an open heart and words of confession, He is just and will forgive us of all unrighteousness. With this emptying of your old self, God will give you hymns of praise and a new song, one written just for you.

One way God's new song of joy is heard is through laughter, and the home is an important place for laughter to be heard. In his poem "Laughter in the Walls," Bob Benson reminds us of the role that laughter can play in our family time:

I pass a lot of houses on my way home—
   some pretty,
      some expensive,
         some inviting—

but my heart always skips a beat
    when I turn down the road
and see my house nestled against the hill.
    I guess I'm especially proud
of the house and the way it looks because
    I drew the plans myself.
It started out large enough for us—
    I even had a study—
two teenaged boys now reside in there.
    And it had a guest room—
my girl and nine dolls are permanent guests.
    It had a small room Peg
had hoped would be her sewing room—
    the two boys swinging on the dutch door
have claimed this room as their own.
    So it really doesn't look right now
as if I'm much of an architect.
    But it will get larger again—
one by one they will go away
    to work,
        to college,
            to service,
                to their own houses,
and then there will be room—
    a guest room,
     a study,
    and sewing room
for just the two of us.
But it won't be empty—
    every corner
        every room
            every nick
                in the coffee table

will be crowded with memories.
Memories of picnics,
    parties, Christmases,
        bedside vigils, summers,
            fires, winters, going barefoot,
    leaving for vacation, cats,
        conversations, black eyes,
    graduations, first dates,
        ball games, arguments,
    washing dishes, bicycles,
        dogs, boat rides,
    getting home from vacation,
        meals, rabbits and
a thousand other things
    that fill the lives
of those who would raise five.
And Peg and I will sit
    quietly by the fire
    and listen to the
    laughter in the walls.[20]

When the children are gone and you no longer have to
go to work, what will you hear as you sit in your house? I
hope it's laughter, for God created laughter for you and your
family to share.

*Father God, let me take time to build memories
of laughter and fun with my family. Fill me with
Your joy so that I may be remembered not as solemn
or angry but as joyful in You. May my laughter echo
strong in the walls long after I'm gone. Amen.*

Taking Action

❖ Buy a clean joke book and tell a new joke at the dinner table for one week. Begin to laugh more at home.

❖ Pass the book on to another member of the family and let that person tell a joke at dinner each night next week.

❖ Your kids will only be home for a short period of your life. What will you start doing to create more laughter in the walls of your home?

❖ Rediscover and nurture the "child" inside of you. It's the key to your creativity, sense of wonder and of joy.

❖ Rent a funny video and have a "Laugh-In" party. Admission is free with a joke and be sure to have some good snacks. Encourage everyone to laugh loudly. Stop the film and rewind to see some of the funny parts again.

Reading On
Habakkuk 3:17-18   Luke 15:8-10   Acts 2:46-47

Do not neglect to show hospitality to strangers, for by this some have entertained angels without knowing it.

— *Hebrews 13:2* NASB

We Do What We Want to Do

Scripture Reading: Genesis 18:18-19

Key Verse: Genesis 18:19

> *For I have chosen him, so that he will direct his children and his household after him to keep the way of the Lord by doing what is right and just, so that the Lord will bring about for Abraham what he has promised him.*

My parents spent a lot of time with me, and I wanted my kids to be treated with as much love and care as I got. Well, that's a noble objective. Everyone feels that way. But to translate it into daily life, you really have to work at it.

There's always the excuse of work to get in the way of the family. I saw how some of the guys at Ford lived their lives— weekends merely meant two more days at the office. That wasn't my idea of family life. I spent all my weekends with the kids and all my vacations. Kathi was on the swim team for seven years, and I never missed a meet. Then there were tennis matches. I made all of them. And piano recitals. I made all of them too. I was always afraid that if I missed one, Kathi might finish first or finish last and I would hear about it secondhand and not be there to congratulate—or console—her.

People used to ask me: "How could somebody as busy as you go to all those swim meets and recitals?" I just put them down on my calendar as if I were seeing a supplier or a dealer that day. I'd write down: "Go to country club. Meet starts at three-thirty, ends four-thirty." And I'd zip out.[21]

We face many choices every day of our life. In order to be sure that we're choosing what is most important, we need to reconfirm each day what is of greatest value to us. We also need to look to the Lord for His direction.

What are you doing to be directed by God? Do you have a teachable spirit? Are you honestly seeking His will for you in the little details as well as the big issues of life? Ask God each day to help you choose to do what is right and just. We all do what we want to do, so ask Him to help you want to do what He wants you to do. When you follow in His ways, then the Lord will bring about for you what He has promised you.

Today's key verse points out the reward of following God's ways in our family: again, the Lord says He will bring about what He has promised. In Proverbs 24:3-4 we learn more about these promises: "By wisdom a house is built, and through understanding it is established; through knowledge its rooms are filled with rare and beautiful treasures." Is the writer of Proverbs talking about furniture, carpets, crystal vases, and fine paintings? I don't think so. Instead, these rare and beautiful treasures God promises are God-fearing, God-respecting children, with godly values, who honor their mother and father and respect other people. God has promised these rewards and blessings if we follow His instructions.

Are you following those instructions? What choices are you making? What are you doing with your life? Ask God today to give you a new passion for following His directions and for making His choices in your life.

> *Father God, let me build my house with wisdom, establish it with understanding, and through knowledge fill its rooms with rare and beautiful treasure— children who know You, love You and serve You.... Help me live so that my wife and children are a top priority of life.... Also, give me a teachable spirit and reveal to me today how I can live according to Your ways. Amen.*

Taking Action

❖ What specific instructions does God give you for raising your children? Write them down.

❖ Beside each God-given instruction that you listed, state specifically what you plan to do to act on these instructions.

❖ List a few of the blessings that God has so abundantly given you.

❖ A hundred years from now the size of your bank account won't matter, nor the size or style house you live in, nor the model car you drive. But the world may be different because you were deeply involved in the lives of your children. Looking at your life from this perspective, what changes do you want to make?

Reading On

Proverbs 27:17	Proverbs 22:6
Proverbs 20:11	Proverbs 19:18

> Winning is not a sometime thing; it's an all-time thing. You don't win once in a while, you don't do things right once in a while, you do them right all the time. Winning is a habit. Unfortunately, so is losing.
>
> — *Vince Lombardi*

Seven Habits to Cultivate to Be an Effective Christian

❖ *Solitude* — Give top priority to your relationship with God.

❖ *Study* — Only when you're studying and applying God's truth in the Bible can you discern what's right or wrong, true or false, loving or cruel, profitable or foolish, noble or cowardly.

❖ *Support* — Find three or four other Christian men and humbly say to them, "Help me grow—and let's grow together."

❖ *Celebration* — Knowing that this world can weigh us down and wear us out, God encourages us to take and make time for celebrating.

❖ *Prayer* — Devote a set period of time each day to meet with the Lord in prayer. Take time to adore His greatness, confess your sins, thank Him for all He has given you, and lay before Him your concerns and burdens.

❖ *Simplicity* — Keep your life simple. Learn to cut back on your commitments.

❖ *Compassion* — Look out for the interests of others. You can't solve all the world's problems, but you can — and are called to — help those whom God has placed in your life.

God's Rewards

Scripture Reading: Matthew 19:27-20:16

Key Verse: Matthew 19:29

> *"Everyone who has left houses or brothers or sisters or father or mother or children or fields for my sake will receive a hundred times as much and will inherit eternal life."*

Why do you do what you do? Through the years, I've asked myself again and again, "Why do I serve? What is my motivation for speaking, writing, giving to the church, being a father, and loving my wife and family?" Put more bluntly, "What will I get as a result of my efforts?"

You've probably asked the same question. I know my employees did whenever I offered them promotions. Most would ask, "How much more money will I make?" and "Will there be any increase in health insurance, vacations, bonuses, retirement, etc.?" Basically, they wanted to know, "What's in it for me?" And in today's passage, Peter asks Jesus the same question when he says, "What then will there be for us?"

Jesus answers Peter's question and tells him—and us—what's in it for us when we serve God and His kingdom:

- Whatever we give up we will receive a hundred times as much.

———— ❖ ————

- We will inherit eternal life.

- Many who are first will be last, and many who are last will be first.

These rewards are gracious and generous, but are you letting these rewards motivate your service to God? Or do you, like many people, think instead that God will punish you if you don't serve Him?

Each day I ask God to first reveal to me my true motivation in serving Him and then to purify my reasons. I ask Him to help me accept the rewards promised in His Word and to serve not just because I fear His punishment. Do you believe that God graciously promises not only eternal life because we have accepted Jesus as Lord and Savior but also to give us a hundredfold return on all we have given up to serve Him?

Take a moment to, as the old hymn says, "Count your blessings and name them one by one." Some of the ones on my list are knowing Jesus face-to-face, my salvation, my family, a nice home, a worthwhile ministry, good health, our church, our pastor.... The list continues, each item reminding me that God does indeed take care of His people when they sacrifice to serve Him.

Today's Scripture reading also teaches that "the last shall be first." You and I try hard to be fair in our dealings with other people, and this passage can seem unfair from our human perspective. The farmer wants to give the man who was hired last the same he gave to workers who had been there longer (Matthew 20:14). Why would a farmer pay the late worker the same amount as the early worker who had been in the fields all day? The farmer here represents God, whose amazing grace and generosity know

❖

no bounds. It is irrelevant that we as men might feel the farmer's actions are wrong or, from our perspective, unfair. God chooses to do what He chooses to do.

So are you willing to serve God? He will reward us generously whether we go to the field at three o'clock in the afternoon or have been there since early morning.

Father God, search me and show me my motivation for what I do. Forgive my selfishness. Give me a pure heart that joyfully and energetically serves You, the Author and Giver of life. Help me serve with my eyes on You and not on other people, hoping that they'll notice what I do. And thank You for the gracious and generous rewards You promise even when our motives aren't pure and our service is imperfect. Amen.

Taking Action

❖ Answer the question that opens today's selection—"Why do you do what you do?"

❖ Now list at least 10 blessings. What does this list show you about God?

❖ Where is God calling you to serve? What will you do in response?

Reading On

Matthew 6:33   Mark 10:29-31

Wealthy Men

The men who have pride and peace of mind
And the respect of other men...
The men who say in their twilight years
That they'd do it all again...
The men who love the flowers and trees
And watching the animals play...
These are wealthy men, for what they have
Can never be taken away.

— George E. Young

Know Your Children

Scripture Reading: Proverbs 22:1-16

Key Verse: Proverbs 22:6

> *Train a child in the way he should go, and when he is old he will not turn from it.*

———— ❖ ————

As I look at our grandchildren, Christine, Chad, Bevan, and Bradley Joe II, I see four unique people and find myself face-to-face with the challenge of understanding each of them so that I can help mold a godly character in them. Fortunately, each of them wants to be known. In fact, each one of us—whatever our age—wants people to take time to know us, to appreciate how we're different from everyone else, and to recognize our likes, our dislikes, and the things about us that make us who we are.

In raising our own children, Emilie and I saw a lot of differences between Jenny and Brad, and those differences are still there. Recognizing these differences early on, we realized that we had to teach, motivate, and discipline each of them according to their personality. God helped us understand that children need to be trained in a way tailor-made for them personally.

The first word in today's key verse is the word "train." In the Hebrew, this word originally referred to the roof of the mouth and the gums. In Bible times, the midwife would stick her finger into a sweet substance and then place it into

154

the new baby's mouth to get the infant sucking. She would then hand the child to its mother, and the child would start nursing. This was the earliest form of "training." We need to keep in mind, though, that the word "child" in today's text can be a newborn up through a person of marrying age. The trick to get the baby nursing was only the first step in a long period of training.

And, according to the verse, the value of this training is so that "when he is old he will not turn from it." In Hebrew, this word for "old" means "bearded" or "chin." Solomon is talking about a young man who begins to grow a beard, and that can be as early as junior high or as late as college. The idea Solomon communicates is that we parents are to continue training our children as long as they are under our care—and we are to train our children God's way, not according to our ideas, our ways, or our plans.

It's important to see that this verse is not a guarantee to parents that raising children God's way means that they will never stray from His path. But our efforts to train our children to follow God will be most effective when we use the methods most appropriate to their unique personality. We need to approach each child differently and not compare them to one another. We need to appreciate that fact that each child is uniquely made. We need to be a student of our children.

It was easy to see that Jenny was not Brad and that Brad certainly wasn't Jenny. And like Jenny and Brad, each child has his or her own bent, already established by our Creator God when He places them in our family. God has given you unique children. Get to know them.

*Father God, thank You for the children You
have placed in my care. Help me to know each of*

them well. Give me insight into their unique personalities, patience so I can understand them, and wisdom to know how to teach them. Help me to build them up to be all that You designed them to be. Amen.

Taking Action

❖ In what ways are your children different from you? Different from each other? Be specific.

❖ In light of the differences between your children you've identified, how will you train them differently? What approach will you take with each?

❖ Learn one new thing about each of your children today. Then do something with that information.

❖ Tell your child today one thing you appreciate about him/her that makes him/her special to you.

Reading On
Psalm 139:13-16

In the day of my trouble I shall call upon Thee, for Thou wilt answer me.

— *Psalm 86:7* NASB

The Language of Love

Scripture Reading: 1 Corinthians 13:4-13

Key Verse: 1 Corinthians 13:4

Love is patient, love is kind. It does not envy, it does not boast, it is not proud.

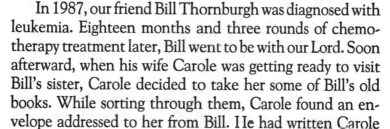

In 1987, our friend Bill Thornburgh was diagnosed with leukemia. Eighteen months and three rounds of chemotherapy treatment later, Bill went to be with our Lord. Soon afterward, when his wife Carole was getting ready to visit Bill's sister, Carole decided to take her some of Bill's old books. While sorting through them, Carole found an envelope addressed to her from Bill. He had written Carole an Easter card two years earlier, and she had tucked it away in a book. Rediscovering the card, she thanked God for her husband's written words.

At Christmastime in 1989, Carole had this Easter message from her husband. It read:

A Tearful Week
A Long Week
A Hard Week
A Lonely Week
A Painful Week
A Revealing Week
A Recovering Week

A Reassuring Week
A Peace Week
A Rededication Week
A Friendship Week
A Love Week
A Roller Coaster Week
A Renewal Week
A Glorious Week
A Victorious Week
A Life-Changing Week
But A Week I Will Never Lose Sight Of
    May God be our source of true love and friendship. You have been so good these days. I love you for it. You have been all a husband would desire. Forgive me, Sweet, for not keeping our love fresh. I love you.
    Happy Easter and Happy Beginnings,

Bill

    Bill's words offered Carole a comforting sense of his presence after he was gone. But even when he was alive, Bill and Carole spoke openly of their love for one another. Do you and your wife?
    We husbands would do well to learn the language of love. We need to practice saying, "I love you." We need to say those words, but we also need to speak them through our sensitivity to our spouse, our actions, and our conversation. If I'm going to run some errands, for instance, I can ask Emilie if there's anything I can get for her while I'm out. I can let her know I'm listening to her by turning off the television or putting down the paper. I can also show Emilie that I love her with an evening at the theater, a new dress, a gift certificate for a dress, a pair of shoes, a massage, a weekend in Palm Springs—whatever would be a treat for

her. However I choose to show my love, I say aloud to Emilie, "Just another way to say, 'I love you!' " Acts of kindness like this are powerful and effective ways to strengthen your friendship with your mate. Such thoughtfulness shows your wife that you do not take her for granted.

Emilie and I also rely on certain family rituals and traditions to give us an opportunity to express our love for one another. We kiss each other goodnight and say, "May God bless your sleep." We celebrate our love on anniversaries and birthdays by giving each other small gifts. We telephone one another when we're apart, visit one of our favorite restaurants on special occasions, go out to lunch, attend the theater, and share hugs and (my contribution) corny jokes. All of these things—spontaneous little acts as well as carefully planned events—are ways to show your wife you love her.

One word of caution! Be sure that you are expressing your love in the language—in the words and the actions—that your spouse will understand as love! Just because you feel loved when she plans a special dinner out doesn't mean that she feels loved when you do the same for her. Be a student of your wife. Know what best communicates to her the love you have. And keep your eyes open for common, everyday events that give you the chance to express that love.

I continually strive to make sure that our love is patient, kind, that it does not envy, does not boast, or is not proud. It's a lifetime of challenges in developing a Christlike expression of love one to another. Jerry and Barbara Cook offer another way to tell your wife that you love her:

I Need You

I need you in my times of strength and in my weakness;
I need you when you hurt as much as when I hurt.
There is no longer the choice as to what we will share.
We will either share all of life or be fractured persons.
I didn't marry you out of need or to be needed.
We were not driven by instincts or emptiness;
We made a choice to love.
But I think something supernatural happens at the point
    of marriage commitment (or maybe it's actually
    natural).
A husband comes into existence; a wife is born.
He is a whole man before and after, but at a point in
    time he becomes a man who also is a husband;
That is— a man who needs his wife.
She is a whole woman before and after.
But from now on she needs him.
She is herself but now also part of a new unit.
Maybe this is what is meant in saying, "What God hath
    joined together."
Could it be He really does something special at "I do"?
Your despair is mine even if you don't tell me about it.
But when you do tell, the sharing is easier for me;
And you also can then share from my strength in that
    weakness.[22]

*Father God, I want my wife to know that I love
her. Teach me to be more open about my feelings.
Help me be a student of my wife so that I know what
actions and words make her feel loved. Amen.*

Taking Action

❖ Do something for your wife that you hate doing but she loves—watching a romantic movie or going shopping when your favorite ball game is on TV.

❖ Send her flowers.

❖ Give her a certificate for a massage.

❖ Take care of the children while she goes on the church's women's retreat.

❖ Go out for coffee with your wife and talk about the day.

Reading On

1 Peter 4:7-11   1 John 4:7-21

There's Something About That Name

Scripture Reading: Isaiah 9:6-7

Key Verse: Isaiah 9:6b
> *He will be called Wonderful Counselor, Mighty God,*
> *Everlasting Father, Prince of Peace.*

What do you think of when you hear the name "Jesus"? Miracles? Salvation? Peace? Purpose? Joy? Power? Hope? All of these—and more? There is indeed something about that name, the name of the Almighty God who parted the Red Sea, raised Lazarus from the dead, and lives today in every believer.

And the fact that He lives today gives us hope and peace. As Isaiah wrote, "Of the increase of his government or peace there will be no end" (9:7). Life brings sorrow, broken hearts, health problems, financial difficulties, and many other hardships. But God gives us peace and hope for those times. Let yourself depend on God and find refuge and restoration in Him.

It helps some people to think about putting all their problems and worries in a box, sealing the lid, laying it at Jesus' feet, and then walking away, never turning back. It also helps to realize that 80 percent of the things we worry about never happen anyway— and we can let Jesus take the remaining 20 percent. In response, He will give back to you 100 percent of His life and peace. In fact, He has done it already for you when He hung on the cross of Calvary.

Jesus. There is indeed something about that name—and may you find in the Person it names exactly what you need today.

> *Father God, You have many names. As I search the Scripture, teach me the significance of each name so that I can have a deeper understanding of who You are. Reveal Your character to me. Amen.*

Taking Action

❖ What are you worried about today? What will you let Jesus do about these concerns?

❖ List your blessings one by one. What does this list reveal about God?

❖ Start a list of the various names of God. Add to it whenever you come across another in your reading. Beside each, make a note of why that name is significant to you personally.

Reading On

Philippians 4:8   Psalm 23   Joshua 24:14-15

Let the word of Christ richly dwell within you.

— *Colossians 3:16*

Your Idea of Who God Is

The most portentous fact about any person is not what he at a given time may say or do, but what he in his deep heart conceives God to be like.... A right conception of God is basic to practical Christian living. There is scarcely an error in doctrine or a failure in applying Christian ethics that cannot be traced finally to imperfect and ignoble thoughts about God.

— A.W. *Tozer*

Quite a Father!

Scripture Reading: Matthew 7:7-12

Key Verse: Matthew 7:11

> *If you, then, though you are evil, know how to give good gifts to your children, how much more will your Father in heaven give good gifts to those who ask him!*

Last year when I was at the Dallas/Fort Worth Airport waiting for a flight to California, I purchased a Sunday morning newspaper. While looking through the classified section, I came upon a daughter's tribute to her father.

> This is an open letter to my father which I desire to share with those of you who did not have the privilege of knowing him. J.T. Yates was a war hero of the European Campaign fighting in the Battle of the Bulge. He landed in France on D-Day and fought his way across Europe not only as a medic but also as a combat soldier putting his life in jeopardy constantly while trying to save others. He was a man of his own will and lived his life according to his own beliefs and convictions.

> But he was also a hero to me as only a daughter can know and love a father. He was my teacher, whether it be from learning how to

survive in the wilderness, to catching a fish, planting a garden, writing a school drama, making science projects or caring for animals. Unknowingly he strengthened my admiration and appreciation of him. He was my place of safety whenever he held me and cradled me in his big strong arms. Daddy always tried to give me joy. We made every circus that came to town, walked in every parade, rode in every rodeo, played ball in the park or took many walks through the zoo. Even at home, he would play games with me, tell me stories, or camp out in the yard. Every year at Christmas, Santa would come to our house and sit me on his knee yet not one time did I ever suspect that was my dad. They tried to tell me one time that Santa Claus was make-believe but I knew better. I was fortunate to live with him every day for many years. Daddy always let me shine and have all the glory while he stood behind in the shadows. That was his way.

The world may not have considered him a religious man, but he did believe in God. If he couldn't go to church with me, he always provided me a way. Daddy respected men of the clergy and on Sunday afternoons there was always plenty of food for any of God's people that would visit. His love for children was unsurpassed by no one and there were lots of wiener roasts and entertainment for all youth. That foundation stayed with me and carried me through the next forty years of my life.

Daddy was a man of strong convictions. He never turned his head and pretended not to see.

He would stand up to any man, stand up for any woman, stand with any child and stand behind his beliefs. Daddy was always there when I needed him and his love was always enough.

If he could, he would have spared me pain, cried my tears to protect all sadness from my eyes. If he could, he would have walked with me everywhere I went to make sure I never chose a wrong turn that might bring me harm or defeat. If he could, he would have shielded my innocence from time, but the time he gave me really wasn't his. He could only watch me grow so he could love me for who I was. But Daddy was a wise man. He knew love couldn't be captured or protected. So he let me take my chances, he gave me my freedom, he let me fight my own battles. I made mistakes but he was always patient.

He was the most generous and giving man of his own self I have ever known and I hope the legacy he left me will be passed to multitudes of generations.

Thank you, Daddy, for all the times and all the nurturing you have given me. The memories will always be in my mind. Now that there will be no more rainbows for us, I will have to let you go, Daddy, but I will always love you. Your daughter. Paula Yates Sugg[23]

This man was quite a father, but our verses today teach that our heavenly Father far exceeds the goodness of any earthly father. Unfortunately, many of us did not have fathers who modeled God's goodness or pointed us to Him, and we struggle to this day to trust in the goodness of an unseen heavenly Father. In such cases, walking by faith and not by sight is even harder. But whatever our relationship with our earthly father, we can experience the abundance of God's goodness if we ask Him.

Today would be a great time to take another step toward greater trust in God, your heavenly Father. Go to Him in prayer with thanksgiving and adoration, with your confessions and your petitions. Know that He will meet you where you are and that He is able to meet all your needs far more abundantly than you can imagine (Ephesians 3:20).

> *Father God, teach me to be the father You want me to be. Use me to point my children to You and to encourage my wife in her walk of faith. And help me let You be the kind of father to me that I want to be to my kids so that I may learn from You—for their sake. Amen.*

Taking Action

❖ Write your earthly father a letter expressing your love for him. Don't wait until it's too late.

❖ If your father has passed away, write that letter anyway so that you can express what you've always kept inside.

❖ If your experience with your earthly father wasn't good and you can't write a letter of appreciation and love, you might instead write a letter describing your hurts. Then share the letter with your heavenly Father. Ask Him for wisdom and strength as you raise your children. Let the pain of the past generations stop in your generation.

❖ If you haven't acknowledged your heavenly Father

❖

before, open your heart to Jesus today. Know that God wants you to recognize His Son as Lord and Savior and Himself as your loving and good Father.

Reading On

John 3:16	John 10:10
Romans 3:23	Romans 6:23
Romans 5:8	John 14:6
1 Corinthians 15:3-6	John 1:12
Ephesians 2:8-9	Revelation 3:20

> He shall be the stability of your times, a wealth of salvation, wisdom, and knowledge.
>
> — *Isaiah 33:6*

The Silver Market Just Crashed

Scripture Reading: Proverbs 30:1-14

Key Verse: Proverbs 30:8

> *Give me neither poverty nor riches, but give me only my daily bread.*

───── ❖ ─────

What message does God have for you today? Ask yourself that as you read through author Hank Hanegraaff's account of a life-changing lesson he learned the hard way.

The year was 1979. I had only recently committed my life to Jesus Christ. Although exhilarated by my relationship with the Lord of the universe, I was also haunted by all the wasted years—years of living by the dictates of my own will. I desperately wanted to make up for lost time.

More than anything else, I wanted to make my life count. I felt that to make up for lost time I had to free myself from financial constraints and considerations. And so I decided to take some of the financial resources I had accumulated and parlay them into a small fortune.

The silver commodities market seemed to be

170

the quickest route to financial security. I had been watching its rapid ascent and had been hearing about its potential in the financial markets. My research seemed to indicate that silver was grossly undervalued and that it was just a matter of time until it soared to previously unheard-of heights. Even from a biblical standpoint, it seemed to me that the proper ratio between gold and silver should be 10 to 1.

As I continued to consider using silver as the vehicle to achieve financial security, the market began to heat up. I decided to wait for a price correction so I could get into the market at a reasonable entry level.

Meanwhile, I planned a visit to my parents, who lived in the Netherlands. My motive was to map out a strategy for financial security: I wanted to serve God from a position of strength as a prosperous Christian. But, as I would soon discover, God had a radically different plan for my life.

After several days in Holland, I looked for something to read to pass the time. Since reading Dutch had become cumbersome for me, I was delighted to find a book printed in English on the coffee table in my parents' den. It was titled *Evangelism Explosion*. Once I started reading, I just couldn't stop. Within a few hours I encountered a whole new world— a world of spiritual multiplication. As I read on I began to discover how I could become an equipped Christian and how to store up treasure in heaven.

I returned to the States excited about the

possibility of spiritual multiplication and immediately enrolled in the evangelism outreach program of my local church. However, my desire for financial security continued to burn brightly. Silver prices by this time had begun to skyrocket. Anxious to "get on before the train left without me," I jumped into the market at $47.08 per ounce. Often I would look back and kick myself for not having acted sooner. I would calculate exactly how much I had lost by not acting when I first began to see silver's meteoric ascent. Leveraged to the hilt, I waited anxiously for silver to continue rising. It did. Within a few days it hit the 50-dollar mark and the predictions were that it wouldn't be long before it would crack the century mark (100 dollars per ounce).

Eagerly I waited, fully believing that God would soon allow me to become financially self-sufficient. But within days I received a call that caused my heart to freeze. The voice on the other end of the line said, "Hank, disaster!" Before I could respond he blurted out the chilling words, "The silver market just crashed." I was told to come over immediately to cover the shortfall (a "margin call") or my position in the market would be liquidated. Over the next few months this would become a recurring scene. The phone call would come and I would have to cover another shortfall, always wondering how far I should chase the rabbit down the hole. With each passing week I was losing more and more of what had taken me years to accumulate. Yet in seeking advice from the experts, I was consistently counseled to hang in there—that they were just "shaking the amateurs out of the market."

But something else was happening as well. All the while I was losing financially, I was gaining spiritually. During the on-the-job training portion of Evangelism Explosion I was going into the highways and byways and seeing people come to faith in Christ. On the one hand, I was prospering spiritually to a degree I never dreamed possible.

Eventually I lost everything I had worked so long and hard to possess financially. But spiritually, I was gaining an eternal perspective. I was learning to seek first God's kingdom and His righteousness (Matthew 6:33). I was coming to realize that He would take care of my daily needs. Like Agur in Proverbs 30, I was learning to pray, "Give me neither poverty nor riches, but give me only my daily bread. Otherwise, I may have too much and disown you and say, 'Who is the Lord?' Or I may become poor and steal, and so dishonor the name of my God."

While Scripture neither condemns nor commends riches, the goal spiritually is to grow to such an extent in your relationship with Christ that, as the old hymn says, "the things of earth grow strangely dim in the light of His glory and grace." The bottom line is to develop an eternal rather than a temporary perspective—eyes that can look beyond time and space into eternity.

Today I can only manage a wry smile as I think back and read the words of the apostle Paul to young Timothy: "People who want to get rich fall into temptation and a trap and into many foolish and harmful desires that plunge men into ruin and destruction" (1 Timothy 6:9).[24]

Father God, I echo Agur's prayer and Hank Hanegraaff's prayer. Give me neither poverty nor riches; but give me only my daily bread. Otherwise, I may have too much and let riches be my god. Or I may become poor and desperate and then dishonor Your name.... Reveal to me all that is standing in the way of my devotion to You, Lord.... And teach me to live a life of service that pleases You. Amen.

Taking Action

❖ In your journal, list those things that are keeping you from serving God with your whole heart.

❖ Now, next to each item, state specifically what you will do to remove these barriers.

❖ At the same time that you work to remove these barriers, what steps will you take to serve God more wholeheartedly?

Reading On
Matthew 6:33   1 Timothy 6:9-10
Mark 10:29-30   1 Timothy 4:7-8

Things

To seek your pleasure from things you own
Whether many things or few,
Can add spice to life and bring some joy
Until those things own you.

— *George E. Young*

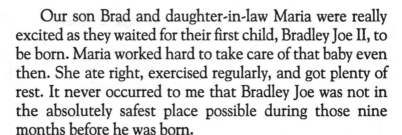

A Child of God

Scripture Reading: John 10:10-18

Key Verse: John 10:10

> *The thief comes only to steal and kill and destroy; I have come that they may have life, and have it to the full.*

———— ❖ ————

Our son Brad and daughter-in-law Maria were really excited as they waited for their first child, Bradley Joe II, to be born. Maria worked hard to take care of that baby even then. She ate right, exercised regularly, and got plenty of rest. It never occurred to me that Bradley Joe was not in the absolutely safest place possible during those nine months before he was born.

Then one evening we attended a service at an Evangelical Free Church in Fullerton, California. Pastor Chuck Swindoll introduced the speaker for the evening, a man by the name of Ravi Zacharias. His opening statement was "The most dangerous place for a young child today is in his mother's womb." He was talking about our country's abortion epidemic. Children are being thrown away like trash, right in our own cities. We as a society no longer view children as "a gift of the Lord" (Psalm 127:3 NASB), much less a miracle of the Almighty God.

After a bout with cancer, our niece Becky and her husband George adopted a son. God allowed a child to be born to another woman so Becky and George could be parents. This child is another a gift from God. He wasn't thrown away in an abortion clinic. Instead, he was adopted into a family who wanted a child.

And that's exactly what God offers us. He wants to adopt us into His family. We are not God's throwaways. We are His much-loved children for whom He sent His Son Jesus to die. Jesus came to give us life (John 10:10) and then went to the cross so that we will never have to suffer the punishment of sin.

Jesus enables us to go before the Almighty God, and that relationship with Him that Jesus makes possible fills the God-shaped void in our spirit. Nothing in the world can fill that vacuum—although we try to fill it with our work, recreation, busyness, toys, sex, alcohol, and many other things. We can experience this spiritual void as mental, emotional, or even physical problems. When those problems help us acknowledge the hunger for God that is at their root, we can find fulfillment, contentment, and the abundant life Jesus promised. Have you let yourself be adopted as God's child? Are you experiencing the abundant life He offers His sons and daughters?

Thank You, Jesus, for showing me Your love by dying for me, a sinner. And thank You for the promise of abundant life. Help me to experience that even now.... And, Lord, help me also to view my children as gifts from You. Forgive me when I'm impatient with them, when I don't make them the priority I want them to be. Make me into the kind of father You want me to be—I pray for the sake of my children. Amen.

Taking Action

❖ Are you a child of God, adopted into His family? If you are, spend some time thanking God for what He did to make that possible. If not, ask Jesus into your heart and life now.

❖ Read the Book of John. Get to know Jesus better.

❖ Pray that God would help you experience the abundant life He offers.

❖ Ask God how He would have you be involved in fighting for the lives of unborn children in our country.

Reading On

John 1:9	Luke 9:23
Mark 9:37	John 1:12

> Delight yourself in the LORD and he will give you the desires of your heart.
>
> — *Psalm 37:4*

Wise and Loving Discipline

Scripture Reading: Proverbs 3:11-12; 13:24; 15:13; 17:22; 22:15; 29:15

Key Verse: Proverbs 15:13

A happy heart makes the face cheerful, but heartache crushes the spirit.

———— ❖ ————

Parenting is an overwhelming task, and how to discipline our kids is one of the most perplexing aspects of the job. Fortunately, as you saw in today's Scripture reading, the Book of Proverbs contains some specific verses which offer good biblical principles for raising our children.

We often feel we are in a tug-of-war between child and parent. When the battle has worn us out, the natural tendency is to want to throw in the towel and give up. And far too often parents do in fact give up on the challenge of gently yet firmly shaping their child's will, as a trainer would a wild animal or a potter would a piece of clay. In his book *The Strong-Willed Child*, Dr. James Dobson offers this insight:

> It is obvious that children are aware of the contest of wills between generations, and that is precisely why the parental response is so important. When a child behaves in ways that are disrespectful or harmful to himself or others, his hidden purpose is often to verify the stability of

179

the boundaries. This testing has much the same function as a policeman who turns doorknobs at places of business after dark. Though he tries to open doors, he hopes they are locked and secure. Likewise, a child who assaults the loving authority of his parents is greatly reassured when their leadership holds firm and confident. He finds his greatest security in a structured environment where the rights of other people (and his own) are protected by definite boundaries.[25]

It takes godly wisdom to provide this kind of security for children. How do we set and maintain stable boundaries for them? First, we must note the difference between abuse and discipline. Proverbs 13:24 tells us that if we truly love our children, we'll discipline them diligently. Abuse is unfair, extreme, and degrading. Such action doesn't grow out of love; it springs from anger and hate. Abuse results in a child's damaged self-image, and that damage will often last a lifetime. Discipline, on the other hand, upholds the child's worth; it is fair and appropriate to the infraction.

Second, we must be sure the child understands the discipline he or she is to receive. When we disciplined Jenny and Brad, we spent a lot of time discussing with them what they did. We wanted to make sure they understood what the infraction was. On occasion when a sterner approach was necessary, we did give spankings. They were firmly applied to the beefy part of the buttocks, and they did hurt. Spankings were few and far between, though, and when they did occur, they were never given in anger. And afterwards, we talked again with the children about why they were disciplined and how they would behave differently in the future.

One of the main purposes of discipline in our home was to have the child realize that he was responsible for his actions and would be held accountable for his behavior. Since every child is different, the methods of discipline will vary according to temperament. (In our day, we didn't have "Time Out." However, we've found this to be a very good technique, and we use it with our grandchildren very effectively.) Whatever the type of discipline the infraction warranted, we always ended with prayer, warm hugs, and assuring words about how much we loved our child. This kind of correction strengthens a child's self-image. And clearly defining the boundaries adds to the child's sense of security. Our love for our kids— carefully communicated even in moments of discipline— motivated them to behave according to our family's standards of behavior.

Third, when we discipline our children, we want to shape and not crush their spirit. As Proverbs 15:13 teaches, you can tell by looking in the eyes of children those who are being crushed and those being firmly but lovingly shaped. Our goal as parents is to provide our children with solid direction and self-assurance that will see them through life. The child who is shaped with loving and firm discipline will have a love for life, but a child whose spirit has been crushed has no hope for the future.

Fourth, our discipline must be balanced. We don't want to be so rigid that we don't allow our kids to make mistakes or so loose that they are bouncing off the walls trying to find the boundaries. Children must know where the boundaries are and what the consequences are if they choose to go beyond these limits.

In Scripture we read about physical discipline. The

writer of the Proverbs says, for instance, "Folly is bound up in the heart of a child; but the rod of discipline will drive it far from him" (Proverbs 22:15). Of course none of us wants to risk being an abusive parent, but hear what Dr. Dobson says about the importance of a child being able to associate wrongdoing with pain:

> If your child has ever bumped his arm against a hot stove, you can bet he'll never deliberately do that again. He does not become a more violent person because the stove burnt him; in fact, he learned a valuable lesson from the pain. Similarly, when he falls out of his high chair or smashes his finger in the door or is bitten by a grumpy dog, he learns about physical dangers in his world. These bumps and bruises throughout childhood are nature's way of teaching him what to fear. They do not damage his self-esteem. They do not make him vicious. They merely acquaint him with reality. In like manner, an appropriate spanking from a loving parent provides the same service. It tells him there are not only physical dangers to be avoided but he must steer clear of some social traps as well (selfishness, defiance, dishonesty, unprovoked aggression, etc.).[26]

Fifth, as you discipline your children, be consistent in your approach. Here are some guidelines:

- Make sure there is a clear understanding of the rules.

- Discipline in private. If you're in a public setting, wait until you can be alone.

- Review the infraction and its consequences.

- Be firm in your discipline.

- Assure your child of your love and concern.

- Hug your child after each disciplinary moment.

- End your session with a time of prayer. (Give your child an opportunity to pray, too.)

As Emilie and I look back over our child-raising years, we realize that we made plenty of mistakes. But when we did, we tried always to admit them to our children. So, even though you'll miss the mark occasionally, be sure that you are moving in the proper direction of discipline administered in love. Know that your children want to know their boundaries. Setting and enforcing clear boundaries is a gift of love to them that results in security and self-assurance they can carry through life.

> *Father God, You know that I want for my children what's best for them. Give me the patience to get to know each of my children individually and then grant me the wisdom to know what kind of discipline will be most effective for each. Help me be an effective father who is able to train my children to love and serve You. Amen.*

Taking Action

❖ Do you have a clear direction regarding the goal of your children's discipline? If not, spend some time today thinking about it and write down some of your ideas.

❖ If you're married, you may want to review these ideas with your mate.

❖ Tell each member in your family today that you love them and give a few reasons why.

❖ Take a poll tonight at dinner. Ask each family member, "What's the best thing that happened to you today?" The answers will give you some insight into your children. (Parents must participate, too!)

Reading On

Mark 12:28-31   1 Peter 5:5-6
Galatians 5:16   Colossians 3:17

For as the heavens are higher than the earth, so are My ways higher than your ways, and My thoughts than your thoughts.

— *Isaiah 55:9*

"I Didn't Believe It Anyway"

Scripture Reading: John 6:35-40

Key Verse: John 6:40

For my Father's will is that everyone who looks to the Son and believes in him shall have eternal life, and I will raise him up at the last day.

———— ❖ ————

Emilie and I arrived at our hotel after flying from California to Hartford, Connecticut. It was our first holiday seminar for the season, and the church put us up at a beautiful Ramada Inn. We were anxious to see the turning of the leaves for the first time, and they were at their peak in early October.

We registered at the hotel and went directly to our room. After the airport waits, plane layovers, delays, cramped seating, and heavy luggage, we just wanted to sleep. We turned off the lights at about 9:30 p.m.

Two and a half hours later we were awakened by what we thought was a smoke alarm. I picked up the phone to call the front desk while Emilie looked out the peephole in the door. She couldn't see any smoke, but I wasn't getting an answer from the front desk. As I let the phone ring and ring, the alarm got louder. When Emilie looked out the peephole again, she saw a man running down the hall

185

pulling his pants and jacket on. "Bob, it's a fire!" Emilie yelled. "People are evacuating the building."

I quickly hung up, threw on some clothes, grabbed our briefcases, and quickly left the room. By now, many other guests were doing the same. The alarm was still blasting, and we heard sirens from the fire trucks heading for the hotel. As we walked toward the stairs to hurry down six flights, people pushed through to get ahead. One lady kept yelling, "Hurry, Ruth! Hurry, Ruth!" But Ruth just couldn't move as fast as the others.

We finally made it out into the very chilly, 34-degree midnight air. The entire hotel had been evacuated onto the street, and firefighters were everywhere—only to find out it was a false alarm. We all headed back to our rooms.

As we got off the elevator on our floor, a little lady opened the door to her room just enough to look out and ask, "Was it a fire?"

"False alarm," we answered.

"Well, I didn't believe it anyway."

Crawling back into bed, Emilie and I realized how that woman's words echo the feelings of so many people at Jesus' first coming— "I didn't believe it anyway." How many people heard the message, saw Jesus, witnessed His miracles—and still didn't believe?

The message is clear today: Jesus lives. The Bible tells us the truth about God's plan for salvation, Jesus' role in that plan, and the response to that plan which leads to eternal life. Today's Scripture reading tells us to believe and we will receive eternal life. But today—like 2,000 years ago—many people say, "I didn't believe it." One day it will be too late to choose to believe.

Father God, You know where my heart is hard toward Your message, hard toward You. Forgive me...and work in me to soften my heart. Give me the simple faith of a young child. Let me set aside the sophistication and doubts of adults.... And, Lord, give me the enthusiasm of a young child that I may share the gospel message with others that they might come to believe. Amen.

Taking Action

❖ Share with a friend how you came to believe in Christ.

❖ Emilie concludes her holiday seminars with this poem. What is God saying to you through these lines?

'Twas the Night Before Jesus Came

'Twas the night before Jesus came and all through the
    house
Not a creature was praying, not one in the house.
Their Bibles were lain on the shelf without care
In hopes that Jesus would not come there.

The children were dressing to crawl into bed,
Not once ever kneeling or bowing a head.
And Mom in her rocker and baby on her lap
Was watching the Late Show while I took a nap.

When out of the East there arose such a clatter,
I sprang to my feet to see what was the matter.
Away to the window I flew like a flash
Tore open the shutters and threw up the sash!

When what to my wondering eyes should appear
But angels proclaiming that Jesus was here.
With a light like the sun sending forth a bright ray
I knew in a moment this must be THE DAY!

The light of His face made me cover my head.
It was Jesus! Returning just like He had said.
And though I possessed worldly wisdom and wealth,
I cried when I saw Him in spite of myself.

In the Book of Life which He held in His hand
Was written the name of every saved man.
He spoke not a word as He searched for my name;
When He said, "It's not here," my head hung in shame.

The people whose names had been written with love
He gathered to take to His Father above.
With those who were ready He rose without a sound
While all the rest were left standing around.

I fell to my knees, but it was too late;
I had waited too long and thus sealed my fate.
I stood and I cried as they rose out of sight;
Oh, if only I had been ready tonight.

In the words of this poem the meaning is clear;
The coming of Jesus is drawing near.
There's only one life and when comes the last call
We'll find that the Bible was true after all! [27]

Reading On
    2 Timothy 3:16   Acts 13:38-39

Finding Favor in God's Eyes

Scripture Reading: Genesis 6:8-22
Key Verses: Genesis 6:8,22
Noah found favor in the eyes of the Lord.... Noah did everything just as God commanded him.

If you were to pick up today's paper, you'd probably find a story about someone being honored for something he or she did. The accomplishment of someone in government, sports, medicine, education, theater, or music is being acknowledged by peers or even the world in general. Man finding favor with man is not unusual.

Have you ever thought about how much richer it would be to have God find favor with you? It's awesome to think of our holy God finding favor in us human beings, but He does. And today's reading gives us an example.

Noah lived in a sin-filled world much like ours today. (We human beings haven't changed much over the centuries— we just call "sin" something else.) Despite the wickedness around him, Noah lived a godly life that was pleasing to God.

It's important to realize that Noah didn't find favor because of his individual goodness, but because of his faith in God. You and I are judged by that same standard— are we faithful and obedient to God?

Although Noah was upright and blameless before God,

he wasn't perfect. Genuine faith is not always perfect faith. But despite his human failings, Noah walked with God (verse 9). The circumstances of Noah's life could have blocked his fellowship with God, but his heart qualified him to find favor with God.

Are you seeking favor with God or the favor and honor of men? Noah wanted only to please God. Know that, when you go to God and admit that you are a sinner, you are pleasing God. At that time, you find God's grace and move into a closer relationship with Jesus Christ. May you take steps like this to, like Noah, find favor in God's sight.

> *Father God, what an honor for Noah to have found favor in Your eyes! Help me to be faithful and obedient to You so that You might find favor with me. Give me a renewed hunger for Your Word so that I will know what You want from me and then help me be faithful to Your commands. Amen.*

Taking Action

❖ What can you do to find favor in God's eyes? What kind of person can you be to find favor in His eyes?

❖ If you don't think your life finds favor with God, what changes do you want to make? What steps will you take—and what step will you take today?

❖ What will you do to know God's Word better? Who will you find to hold you accountable to obeying God's Word?

Reading On

John 3:16	Philippians 2:12-15
James 4:6	Psalm 19:14

Speak Out!

Scripture Reading: Romans 1:1-17

Key Verse: Romans 1:16

I am not ashamed of the gospel, because it is the power of God for the salvation of everyone who believes; first for the Jew, then for the Gentile.

———— ❖ ————

Ashamed of the gospel of Christ! Let the skeptic, let the wicked profligate, blush at his deeds of darkness, which will not bear the light, lest they should be made manifest; but never let the Christian blush to own the holy gospel. Where is the philosopher who is ashamed to own the God of Nature? Where is the Jew that is .ashamed of Moses? or the Moslem that is ashamed of Mahomet? and shall the Christian, and the Christian minister, be ashamed of Christ? God forbid! No! Let me be ashamed of myself, let me be ashamed of the world, and let me blush at sin; but never, never, let me be ashamed of the gospel of Christ! [28]

Dr. R. Newton was passionate in his cry. We who name Jesus our Lord and Savior should never be ashamed of the gospel. The apostle Paul certainly never hesitated to share

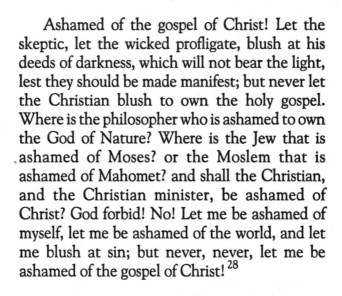

the gospel— and at far greater risk than you and I can imagine. In today's reading, the apostle sets forth seven principles about the gospel. Getting these down can help you and me be bolder in our witness for God's Good News.

Point I: We are "set apart for the gospel" (verse 1). How can that truth help you establish your daily priorities? It's not family, work, finances, politics, or sports that goes to the top of the list. It's the gospel— the love and forgiveness of God made manifest in the birth, life, and death of Jesus Christ— that is to be the focus and guiding principle for your day.

Point II: This gospel was "promised beforehand through His prophets in the Holy Scriptures" (verse 2). The gospel we are commanded to share with those who have never heard it is rooted in history, and that history is documented in the Bible. Our faith is not something recently thought up by a group of men in a back room.

Point III: We are to share the gospel with our whole heart (verse 9). With a passion greater than our zeal for the hometown team, we are to share the news of Jesus Christ with our family, friends, neighbors, and acquaintances.

Point IV: We are to share this good news with everyone (verses 14-15). Paul says he was obligated and eager to preach this gospel to both the Greeks and non-Greeks, to the wise and to the foolish, to everyone. And we are to follow Paul's example. The message of Jesus can make a difference in anyone's life.

Point V: We are to take a stand for the gospel (verse 16). Paul forcefully states, "I am not ashamed of the gospel." Can you and I do the same? We need to stand strong in and for our faith, unashamed of the One who died for our sins and willing to love and serve as He did.

Point VI: We need to see the power of the gospel for salvation (verse 16). The gospel of Jesus Christ is an agent of change. He alone gives real purpose and meaning to life. He alone can help us find victory in our struggle against the power of sin. He alone can transform and heal us. Each of us needs to share our personal experience of these truths.

Point VII: We are to live a life of righteousness by faith (verse 17). When we study the gospel, the righteousness of God is revealed to us so that we can go out and live a righteous life by the power of the Holy Spirit.

Do you "blush to own the gospel?" Do you hesitate to talk about Jesus and the salvation He offers us? Today's passage gives several reasons to speak out. Let's do so!

> *Father God, give me renewed passion for You and Your gospel truth. Don't let me take for granted the freedom I have to share the gospel. Don't let me rely on others to do the sharing. You know the reasons I hesitate.... Help me overcome them.... Give me boldness when I have an opportunity to tell someone about Jesus. Amen.*

Taking Action

❖ Read a good biography of some people of faith who have gone before you. Where do you see the power of the gospel in their lives?

❖ Whom in your life have you wanted to share the Good News with? Do it!

❖ What can you do to be more aware of opportunities to share the gospel? What can you do to prepare yourself to take advantage of those opportunities?

❖ Thank God for sending Jesus Christ to fulfill the prophecies of the Old Testament. Thank God for your own salvation.

Reading On

2 Timothy 3:16	1 Corinthians 15:1-6
Luke 24:27-32	Hebrews 11:1

> Challenges can be stepping stones or stumbling blocks. It's just a matter of how you view them.
>
> — *Unknown*

Spring A.D. 54

Be on the alert. Stand firm in the faith.
Act like men. Be strong.
Let all that you do be done in love.

— *The Apostle Paul*

It All Starts at Home

Scripture Reading: Genesis 2:20b-25

Key Verse: Genesis 2:23

"This is now bone of my bones and flesh of my flesh; she shall be called 'woman,' for she was taken out of man."

—————— ❖ ——————

In his best-selling book *Straight Talk*, Lee Iacocca talks about the importance of the family:

> My father told me that the best way to teach is by example. He certainly showed me what it took to be a good person and a good citizen. As the old joke has it, "No one ever said on his deathbed, I should have spent more time on my business." Throughout my life, the bottom line I've worried about most was that my kids turn out all right.
>
> The only rock I know that stays steady, the only institution I know that works, is the family. I was brought up to believe in it—and I do. Because I think a civilized world can't remain civilized for long if its foundation is built on anything but the family. A city, state or country can't be any more than the sum of its vital parts— millions of family units. You can't have a country or a city or a state that's worth

[anything] unless you govern within yourself in your day-to-day life.

It all starts at home.[29]

In our Scripture reading today we are reminded that God Himself established the family. Although today's secular world is trying its hardest to downgrade the family as an institution, we know that God will not abandon the good work He has begun in the family structure He created (Philippians 1:6).

The Bible is very clear in its teaching that woman was created for man; she is to be his helper. The Bible also clearly teaches that man and woman are designed for each other. These are key elements in God's plan for His people. Do you have a plan for your family? Have you and your mate taken time to determine what values you want to instill in your children and what guidelines you will give them as they grow?

Marriage causes a man to leave his mother and father, be united with his wife, and become one flesh with her. Is this a description of what has happened to you?

Scripture then states, "The man and his wife were both naked, and they felt no shame." Nakedness isn't always physical; it also includes emotional, spiritual, and psychological aspects of who we are. And one of the biggest challenges for Emilie and me is to stand before each other naked and unashamed. If we are following God's plans for our family, we can do just that.

Furthermore, we must follow God's plans for having a healthy family if, as Mr. Iacocca points out, we are to survive as a society. It does all start at home, so let's make it our goal to follow God's plan.

Father God, create in me a hunger to search out Your plan for my life and for my family. Give me the wisdom to major on the majors and not get side-tracked by the minors. It's easy to get distracted from Your plan, but I so want to follow Your master plan for me. When life is over I want You to say, "Well done, good and faithful servant." Help me today. Amen.

Taking Action

❖ Meet with your mate and begin to prayerfully design a master plan for your family.

❖ Write this plan down and include specific goals for each family member.

❖ Begin today to raise good children who know and want to serve the Lord.

Reading On

Genesis 18:19

I can do everything through him who gives me strength.

— *Philippians 4:13*

The Home Is
Where It Happens

The home is the greenhouse where godly wisdom is cultivated. The power of consistent Christian living in the context of family relationships is the primary spiritual classroom for authentic Christianity. The home is where the majority of behavioral traits — good and bad — are learned, reinforced and passed along to future generations....

A home is...filled with fragrant and appealing spiritual riches when each member adopts a servant's spirit. Most family arguments and dissension stem from a failure to yield personal rights. A person filled with the Spirit of Christ strongly desires to serve. He does not seek to establish his own emotional turf but freely edifies and encourages other family members through his servant spirit.

— *Charles Stanley*

□ □ □

The Roots of Humility

Scripture Reading: Philippians 2:1-8
Key Verse: Philippians 2:5
Your attitude should be the same as that of Christ Jesus.

Have you heard of the pastor who was given a badge for being the most humble person in the church? The badge was taken back when he wore it!

Humility. It's hard to get a handle on. What exactly is it?

> I stood in the upstairs hallway, looking down over the bannister and waiting for the younger children to come in for their baths. My oldest daughter, taking a piano lesson, was in the living room directly below, and the repetitive melody she was playing echoed through my mind.
>
> I noticed, however, that one of my young sons was trudging slowly up the stairs, head bowed, grubby hands covering his small, dirt-streaked face. When he reached the top, I asked him what was wrong.
>
> "Aw, nothing," he replied.
>
> "Then why are you holding your face in your hands?" I persisted.
>
> "Oh, I was just praying."

Quite curious now, I asked what he was praying about.

"I can't tell you," he insisted, "because if I do, you'll be mad."

After much persuasion I convinced him that he could confide in me and that, whatever he told me, I would not get mad. So he explained that he was praying about a problem he had with his mind.

"A problem with your mind?" I asked, now more curious than ever, wondering what kind of problem a child of six could have with his mind. "What kind of problem?"

"Well," he said, "you see, every time I pass by the living room, I see my piano teacher, and my tongue sticks out."

Needless to say, it was hard to keep a straight face, but I took his problem seriously and assured him that God could, indeed, help him with it.

Later, on my knees beside the bathtub as I bathed this little fellow, I thought how I still struggle with the problem of controlling my mind and my tongue. That afternoon as I knelt to scrub that sturdy little body, the tub became my altar; the bathroom, my temple. I bowed my head, covered my face; and acknowledged that I, like my son, had a problem with my mind and tongue. I asked the Lord to forgive me and to give me more and more the mind and heart and attitude of Christ.[30]

With the media constantly bombarding us with messages about self-esteem, it's easy to be confused about what genuine humility is. Having the mind and heart and attitude of Christ is a good start, and verse 3 of today's passage adds this: "Do nothing out of selfish ambition or vain conceit, but in humility consider others better than yourself."

As we study the life of Christ, we see that His willingness to serve had its roots in His confidence that God loved Him. Jesus found strength and security in knowing how valuable He was to His Father. This knowledge of His Father's love enabled Jesus to serve people and ultimately die for us sinful human beings. Likewise, knowing our value to God is the first step toward true humility.

It's out of strength, not weakness, that we grow in humility. Dr. Bruce Narramore says that humility has three elements:

- Recognition that you need God

- A realistic evaluation of your abilities

- A willingness to serve [31]

Are those three elements in place in your life? Know that they are aspects of humility and therefore key to serving God's kingdom.

> *Father God, You know how self-centered I am. You know how I'm always busy with something and how I hate to be inconvenienced. I need to learn to give myself away to others. Teach me humility. Teach me to serve as Christ did. Amen.*

Taking Action

❖ Do you recognize your need for God? If so, thank God

for that awareness. If not, why not?

❖ Evaluate your abilities. List ten strengths and ten weaknesses. What are you going to do for the kingdom of God with your strengths? What plans do you have for turning your weaknesses into strengths?

❖ In what three capacities or organizations would you be willing to serve? Step forward and volunteer your services in one of these areas this week.

Reading On
Philippians 2:8-9   James 1:26-3:18
Psalm 39:1-13

> I am only one; but still I am one. I cannot do everything, but still I can do something; I will not refuse to do the something I can do.
>
> — *Helen Keller*

Under Reconstruction

The rule is this: Christians are people who remember their own weaknesses and failure. They are under reconstruction. So they offer hope and forgiveness to people who fall and who need Jesus' healing grace and hope.

— *Donald M. Joy*

□ □ □

Under Orders

Scripture Reading: Ephesians 5:21-33, 1 Corinthians 11:2-12

Key Verse: 1 Corinthians 11:3

Now I want you to realize that the head of every man is Christ, and the head of the woman is man, and the head of Christ is God.

———— ❖ ————

It was one of those golden seasons in life when the sun shines unfailingly warm and the wind blows unfailingly gentle. Linda and I were stationed in what was then West Germany, where I was a brigade signal officer in an armored division. We had been married less than three years, and our hearts were wrapped around each other and around our bright-eyed, red-cheeked, seven-month-old son. We didn't have much in the way of possessions, but I already had everything I'd ever wanted in life—a loving wife, a baby son, a challenging job, and an outstanding commander.

The envelope should have been no surprise.

We knew it was coming. We knew it had to come. Why should my heart pound and my blood run cold when I suddenly received what I knew to be inevitable? And yet...how could I ever be ready to get the ultimate orders to Vietnam? Orders sending me far away from my home and family for long, weary months. Orders that might well be sending me to dismemberment, captivity, or death.

Yet isn't this what I was trained for? Isn't this what I was made for? Our nation was at war. What does a soldier do except go into combat?

Six weeks later we were back in Yakima, in my parents' station wagon, riding those few, silent miles to the airport. My thirty-day leave was over. Christmas was over. The golden days were over. Forever? Who could say? As the plane climbed up and away, I looked back over my right shoulder. Just for a moment, the little window framed all that was in my heart. My very life. Standing on the tarmac were my mom, my dad, my wife, and my baby. Tiny figures...soon lost from view as grey tendrils of cloud swallowed the ascending flight. I remember thinking, Why am I doing this? I would rather be doing anything else right now. Of all the places in the world I would rather be, it's the one I'm leaving.

Finally I had to come back to this: I was doing what I was doing for one reason; I had orders. Like the centurion in Jesus' day, I was a man under authority.

I still am.

No, I'm no longer getting envelopes from the Pentagon, but I am no less a man under authority, a man under orders. And if the Lord God has allowed you the unspeakable privilege of being a husband and father, so are you.[32]

You and I are indeed under orders. The Lord of the universe has called us into His service as husband to our wife and father to our children, and in doing so He describes a man's role in the home as "head." That word is His choice, not ours. As Paul wrote, "Christ is the head of every man, the man is the head of a woman, and God is the head of Christ." These orders—found in God's Word—have been delivered, once and for all. We are not asked to lead; we are commanded to lead. It's not an option.

Throughout the Bible, you'll find God's instructions to those under authority— to anyone who is governed, to believers in the church, to wives, to children, to servants or employees, and, yes, to husbands. And God's instructions to all are very clear. We are to:

- Be subject to Christ

- Be subject to one another

- Respect one another

The world will tell you, "You're your own boss. You're not accountable to anyone. Do what you want to do. And be sure people bow to you." But that is not the message of Scripture. We men do have a certain amount of authority, but more importantly we men are under authority. We are under the authority of Jesus Christ.

And if we are to please the One who gives us our orders for life, we have to ask ourselves questions like these:

- Am I loving my wife as myself?

- Am I taking into account her ideas, opinions, and thoughts; her needs, desires, and dreams?

- Are my children responding to my leadership style?

Are they able to talk to me? Do I respect them and show them that respect? Do my children respect me?

- Am I respectful and submissive to my pastor, to civil authority, and to other believers?

Before you and I can ever lead the way God wants us to, we must learn to follow Him in all we do. Only then can we be effective leaders in our home, leaders who encourage our wife and children in their spiritual growth and care for their emotional and physical needs as well. As you consider these orders, hear what Susan Wesley, the wife of Methodist leader John Wesley, said: "There are two things we have to do with the gospel: one is to believe it. The second is to live it." If we don't live out our faith in the One who is our Head, our leadership will fail. Put differently, if we aren't under God's authority, then we cannot be effective in authority. No one will want to follow a leader who is self-centered. After all, when we are self-centered, then we can't be God-centered.

> *Father God, may I learn to live under Your authority. Give me a heart that is submitted to You so that You might teach me to lead with godly authority. Teach me through Your Word and through godly men I know how to make You number one in my life. Only then can I lead my family in the way You have called me to. Amen.*

Taking Action

❖ What does it mean to you, in your day-to-day life, to be a man under authority?

❖ Discuss 1 Corinthians 11:3 and the idea of "headship" with your wife. Take the risk of asking her, "What do I need to do to be a better leader?"

❖ Take one of your children out for breakfast on Saturday and ask what you could do to be a better dad. Take the risk of being transparent and open to suggestions.

Reading On

Romans 5:12-16	Matthew 20:20-28
Matthew 19:3-9	Genesis 2:24-25

We walk by faith, not by sight.

— *2 Corinthians 5:7*

On Being a Man

It is painful, being a man, to have to assert the privilege, or the burden, which Christianity lays upon my own sex. I am crushingly aware of how inadequate most of us are, in our actual and historical individualities, to fill the place prepared for us.

— **C.S. Lewis**

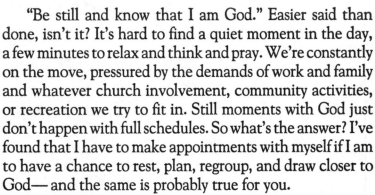

Be Still

Scripture Reading: Psalm 46:1-11

Key Verse: Psalm 46:10

Be still, and know that I am God; I will be exalted among the nations, I will be exalted in the earth.

———— ❖ ————

"Be still and know that I am God." Easier said than done, isn't it? It's hard to find a quiet moment in the day, a few minutes to relax and think and pray. We're constantly on the move, pressured by the demands of work and family and whatever church involvement, community activities, or recreation we try to fit in. Still moments with God just don't happen with full schedules. So what's the answer? I've found that I have to make appointments with myself if I am to have a chance to rest, plan, regroup, and draw closer to God— and the same is probably true for you.

As I write these words, Emilie and I are at a retreat in Laguna Beach, California. It's July, and the temperature is 83 degrees. The weather is perfect, and there's something calming about the waves crashing on the shore. We've spent four days resting and reading. This afternoon, we've talked about family, ministry, food, goals, God's love, His Word, and our writing. Now we're both quiet, and I'm feeling that rare sense of stillness that the psalmist talks about.

It's not often I'm still like this. My life isn't in balance the way I think it should be. I'm still more outwardly focused than inwardly focused. Goals and deadlines, coping with stress, taking care of daily chores, working toward retirement, getting things done—I spend more time and energy on these things than I do praying, meditating on God's Word, listening for His direction, dreaming, and just being with God.

When I was younger, my life was even more out of balance, but as I've gotten older, I find myself doing more of the inward things. I want to glorify God with my life. I want to spend more time alone with Him. I want to get to know Him better, I want Him to use me, and I want to know His peace. And you probably want those things for yourself as well. After all, regular down times—the psalmist's stillness—are as important and necessary as sleep, exercise, and healthy food. But, again, who has the time?

Well, Satan sure doesn't want us to take the time to be still with God. And he doesn't make it easy for us to eliminate the distractions of the job, stress from the boss, family responsibilities, ringing phones, and doing what the kids need. Emilie and I know the battle to make time for rest. So when we set up the year's calendar, we set aside blocks of time to be alone and quiet. In between the speaking engagements, interviews, and travel, we make time for quiet. Our marriage needs it. Our walk with God needs it.

Emilie talks about the door to stillness. And she's right. It's there waiting for any of us to open, but it won't open by itself. We have to choose to turn the knob and make time to enter and sit awhile. Each one of us needs to learn to balance the time we spend in quiet and calm with the time we spend in the fray of everyday existence. Ecclesiastes 3:1 says, "There is a time for everything"—and that includes a time to be still despite our busy life.

> *Father God, life is moving much too fast. The demands never let up and the pressures never ease. I struggle to take a time out. I know I'm more relaxed and can better serve You as husband, father, and worker when I have a daily time with You. Show me how to make that time happen. Amen.*

Taking Action

❖ Read Ecclesiastes 3. What time in life is it for you right now?

❖ If you find it difficult to develop a habit of quiet time, find a prayer partner with the same problem and hold each other accountable.

❖ What will you do to cut down the busyness of your life? What distractions will you eliminate?

Reading On

Isaiah 30:15   Psalm 116:7

Do not love the world or anything in the world. If anyone loves the world, the love of the Father is not in him.

— *1 John 2:15*

Stories to Share

Scripture Reading: Philippians 1:3-11
Key Verse: Philippians 1:3
I thank my God every time I remember you.

Today was a warm, sunny day for January, and two of our four grandchildren were helping us enjoy it. Ten-year-old Christine helped her Grammy Em cook dinner. Bevan and I raked the garden and picked oranges, avocados, and lemons off the trees that surround our house.

As the afternoon progressed, we working men got hot and tired. We were really glad to see Emilie and Christine come up the hill with juice and snacks. We thanked them and headed for the bench that sits under a large shady avocado tree overlooking the grounds and the street in front of our house.

That night, Emilie and I talked about our day with the grandchildren. "What do a PaPa and seven-year-old grandson talk about on a bench under a big avocado tree?" Emilie asked.

"Oh," I replied, "boys talk just like you girls talk—but about boy things."

I had told Bevan, "Someday, when PaPa's in heaven and you drive down this street as a man, you'll look at this bench we are sitting on and remember the day that

Grammy Em and Christine served us jam and toast with a glass of juice."

Then Bevan had said, "Not only will I remember, but I'll bring my son and someday he'll bring his son and point to the bench and tell him about the toast and jam we ate on the bench under that big avocado tree over there."

Only seven years old, Bevan already understood something of the value of one generation sharing stories with the next. What a privilege and responsibility we parents have—to be called to teach our children and grandchildren the story of God's love, the stories of Jesus, so that someday they will thank God for their memory of us and the stories we shared.

> *Father God, thank You for the story of salvation—for the gift of Your Son for my sins. Give me Your words and genuine enthusiasm as I tell that story to my children so that they can come to know and serve You and one day tell their own children about Jesus Christ. Amen.*

Taking Action

❖ What story/stories that your father or grandfather told you do you especially value?

❖ What story/stories do your children or grandchildren like you to tell again and again? (If your list is short, turn to the Bible to add to your repertoire!)

❖ Take a walk with a child. Listen to the stories that he/she has to tell.

❖

Reading On

1 Corinthians 1:4   Deuteronomy 6:7
Psalm 67:1-2

> In matters of style, swim with the current; in matters of principle, stand like a rock.
>
> — *Thomas Jefferson*

The Heat of Life

Scripture Reading: Job 23:1-12

Key Verse: Job 23:10

But he knows the way that I take; when he has tested me, I will come forth as gold.

———— ❖ ————

When times are hard, it's easy to ask, "Why, Lord? Why, Lord, do Your children suffer?" Job certainly had every reason to ask that question. He loved and obeyed God, but God gave Satan permission to test him. That meant great suffering and loss for Job, but he was a man with staying power. One reason his faith in the Lord didn't waver was because his masculinity wasn't determined by what he owned, the size of his home, the amount of his investments, what he could do, the people he knew, the model of donkey he rode, or his status in the community. Job's masculinity and personhood were firmly rooted in who he was, alone and naked, before God. And God is what makes men of all of us.[33]

In that process, God often uses suffering. Our friends Glen and Marilyn Heavilin, for instance, know the kind of suffering Job knew. They have lost three sons—one in a crib death; one twin by pneumonia; and the second twin by a teenage drunk driver. Glen and Marilyn were tested, but they have come through it like gold from a refiner's fire. Today they use their experiences to glorify the name of the Lord.

Marilyn has written five books.[34] Her first, *Roses in December*, was the story of how they lost their sons. Marilyn has had the opportunity to speak all over the country in high school auditoriums filled with teenagers. There she shares her story and talks about life and death, chemical dependency, and God Himself.

Did God know what He was doing when He chose the Heavilins? Of course. They have come forth as gold fired in the heat of life and able to shine for Him. Their pain will never be gone, but they still go forth and minister. They've been very active in "Compassionate Friends," a support group for families who have experienced the death of children. God knew the path the Heavilins would take when they faced their tragic losses, and He's been there as their faith in Him has been purified.

Every one of us has experienced some kind of tragedy. It's not the specifics of the event that matter as much as how we handle it. Today many support groups exist in churches and the community to help you deal with the loss you've faced. A church in Southern California, for instance, has a large group for people who are chemically dependent and their families, and God has used these weekly meetings to change lives. People are talking about their pain and praying together, and many are coming forth as gold. Emilie and I have also visited in a church in Memphis, Tennessee, which started a support group for homosexuals. Many who attend are leaving the gay lifestyle and coming forth as gold.

Whatever loss you're dealing with and however you're

being tested, you can be sure that others have been tested that way, too. So don't go through the testing alone. Find someone through your church who can bear the burden with you. You, too, can and will come forth as gold.

Remember that Jesus Himself knows your pain and that He is always with you and me to help us get through the tough times in life. Trust Him now. It's all part of the coming forth as gold that Job talks about.

> *Father God, it's hard to want to be tested in order to become more like Christ. But I know from my own experience that I rarely grow during the good times and that it's the heat of life that makes our faith like gold. When the fires come, Lord, help me remember that You are there with me. Amen.*

Taking Action

❖ What pain and/or test are you experiencing today?

❖ In a prayer or a letter, let God know how you feel.

❖ How might God be using this in your life to help your faith "come forth as gold"? Be specific.

❖ Find out if there's a support group that could help and make a phone call to find out more about it. The next step will be to attend a meeting.

Reading On

Psalm 66:10   2 Corinthians 4:7-9   Psalm 51:10

Carry each other's burdens, and in this way you will fulfill the law of Christ.

— *Galatians 6:2*

Being a Friend

Scripture Reading: 2 Timothy 1:16-18
Key Verse: 2 Timothy 1:18b

You know very well in how many ways he helped me in Ephesus.

———————— ❖ ————————

In his second letter to Timothy, the apostle Paul writes about Onesiphorus, a man who was a special friend to him. Onesiphorus had "often refreshed" Paul, he had not been ashamed of Paul's chains, and he had searched hard for Paul until he found him. Onesiphorus is the kind of friend we all need—and so is Pythias. Hear his story:

> Damon was sentenced to die on a certain day, and sought permission of Dionysius of Syracuse to visit his family in the interim. It was granted, on condition of securing a hostage for himself. Pythias heard of it, and volunteered to stand in his friend's place. The king visited him in prison, and conversed with him about the motive of his conduct; affirming his disbelief in the influence of friendship. Pythias expressed his wish to die that his friend's honor might be vindicated. He prayed the gods to delay the return of Damon till after his own execution in his stead.

The fatal day arrived. Dionysius sat on a moving throne, drawn by six white horses. Pythias mounted the scaffold, and calmly addressed the spectators: "My prayer is heard: the gods are propitious; for the winds have been contrary till yesterday. Damon could not come; he could not conquer impossibilities; he will be here tomorrow, and the blood which is shed today shall have ransomed the life of my friend. Oh! could I erase from your bosoms every mean suspicion of the honor of Damon, I should go to my death as I would to my bridal. My friend will be found noble, his truth unimpeachable; he will speedily prove it; he is now on his way, accusing himself, the adverse elements, and the gods: but I haste to prevent his speed. Executioner, do your office." As he closed, a voice in the distance cried, "Stop the execution!" which was repeated by the whole assembly. A man rode up at full speed, mounted the scaffold, and embraced Pythias, crying, "You are safe, my beloved friend! I now have nothing but death to suffer, and am delivered from reproaches for having endangered a life so much dearer than my own."

Pythias replied, "Fatal haste, cruel impatience! What envious powers have wrought impossibilities in your favor? But I will not be wholly disappointed. Since I cannot die to save, I will not survive you."

The king heard, and was moved to tears. Ascending the scaffold he cried, "Live, live, ye incomparable pair! Ye have borne unquestionable testimony to the existence of virtue; and that virtue equally evinces the existence of a God to reward it. Live happy, live renowned, and oh! form me by your precepts, as ye have invited me by your example, to be worthy of the participation of so sacred a friendship."

If heathenism had such friendships, what may be expected of Christianity?[35]

What does the world see in your friendships? How is Christ reflected in them? And what are you doing to extend Christian friendship to people who don't yet know the Lord? We have a chance to be a witness for Jesus Christ through our friendships with others, believers and nonbelievers alike.

> *Father God, thank You for the friends I have who, like Onesiphorus did for Paul, stand beside me in all situations, for those friends who are always there when I need them. And, God, teach me to be the kind of friend that Onesiphorus was to Paul. Help me to be alert to the needs of people in my life and then use me to help with those needs. Thank You for giving me opportunities for being a friend. Amen.*

Taking Action

❖ Who needs you to be his Onesiphorus today? What will you do to refresh and encourage him?

❖ Get in touch with a friend you haven't seen for a while.

❖ Let a friend know how much you value him.

Being a Friend

❖

Reading On
Proverbs 18:24   Luke 10:30-37

Your Most
Important Decision

Scripture Reading: Joshua 24:14-15
Key Verse: Joshua 24:15
But as for me and my household, we will serve the Lord.

———— ❖ ————

Some decisions we make in life have eternal consequences, and choosing whom to worship is one such
decision. Thousands of years ago, Joshua faced the same
decision you and I face. Which God will we worship? Will
we—and our families with us—follow the gods of the world
or the one true God?

Joshua was a man of courage, strength, determination,
and faith. He was a leader in his family and in his nation.
And, in today's Scripture reading, this man of God reminds
us that we worship the gods we want to and then boldly
announces that he and his family will serve the Lord.

Which gods are you serving? Poor choices in the past
may be affecting how you answer that question today. If
you're tired of being a slave to poor decisions of the past,
know that you can have freedom in Christ. You can commit
your life to Jesus and let Him turn it around.

Paul writes in Romans 10:9-10 that "if you confess with
your mouth, 'Jesus is Lord,' and believe in your heart that
God raised him from the dead, you will be saved. For it is

with your heart that you believe and are justified, and it is with your mouth that you confess and are saved."

In light of this promise, can you make a decision for Christ today? It will be the best decision of your life. Don't delay. Don't wait until it's too late....

Three times a soldier in a hospital picked up a tract containing the hymn "Will You Go?" Twice he threw it down. The third time, however, he read it, thought about it, and, taking his pencil, wrote deliberately in the margin these words: "By the grace of God, I will try to go, John Waugh, Company G, Tenth Regiment, P.R.V.C." That night, he went to a prayer meeting, read aloud his resolution, requested prayers for his salvation, and said, "I am not ashamed of Christ now; but I am ashamed of myself for having been so long ashamed of him." He was killed a few months later. How timely was his resolution!

Decide now for the first time— or reconfirm an earlier decision— that you and your family will serve the Lord.

> *Father God, each day I must choose what god I will worship. May I, as Joshua did, choose You, Jehovah God. I want to serve You with all my heart and soul. Please renew that desire in me on a daily basis. I love You. Amen.*

Taking Action

- Decide— or decide in an act of recommitment— to serve the Lord. Write today's date in your journal or on the first inside page of your Bible. Also write Romans 8:1 and 1 John 1:9 down for reference.

- Tell a friend of your decision. Ask him to pray for

your spiritual growth and to hold you accountable to serving God and God alone.

Reading On

Romans 3:23	Acts 16:30-31
Romans 6:23	Ephesians 2:8-9

Hold yourself responsible for a higher standard than anyone else expects of you. Never excuse yourself.

— *Henry Ward Beecher*

Reining Your Tongue

Scripture Reading: James 1:19-27

Key Verse: James 1:26

> *If anyone considers himself religious and yet does not
> keep a tight rein on his tongue, he deceives himself and
> his religion is worthless.*

——— ❖ ———

In *All I Really Need to Know I Learned in Kindergarten,*
Robert Fulghum proposes that, in this noisy world of ours,
it's important to have a quiet spirit. He tells of villagers in
the Solomon Islands who felled a tree by screaming at it for
30 days. The tree died, confirming the Islanders' theory that
hollering kills a living thing's spirit. Fulghum then considers
the things that he and his neighbors yell at— the wife, the
kids, the telephone, the lawn mower that won't start,
traffic, umpires, machines. He offers this observation:

> Don't know what good it does. Machines and
> things just sit there. Even kicking doesn't always
> help. As for people, well, the Solomon Islanders
> may have a point. Yelling at living things does
> tend to kill the spirit in them. Sticks and stones
> may break our bones, but words will break our
> hearts.[36]

If we could only remember this each time we want to

yell. Too often, we try to get control over a person or situation by raising our voices. But that is just the opposite of what we need to do. Try lowering your voice next time you're tempted to raise it. See what happens.

The world is full of people dead in spirit because someone didn't realize that loud voices can kill. Try dealing with the situations of life more quietly. Rein your tongue. Let it speak words which arise from a peaceful spirit.

> *Father God, nothing is a greater reminder to me that I, like Paul, do what I don't want to do and don't do what I want to do. You know how I struggle and fail to control my tongue. Forgive me for the hurts I've caused and, Lord, be at work transforming me so that I can learn to rein my tongue. Amen.*

Taking Action

❖ Take some time right now to evaluate how you use your words and your voice in your life. Note those areas where you want to change and, at each one, write out a specific step you will take to make that change.

❖ Today practice lowering your voice when you feel like raising it.

❖ Either in person, by phone, or in a letter, apologize to someone to whom you have talked too harshly.

Reading On

Ephesians 4:29   Matthew 7:15-20

John 15:1-9

"I'm Special Because..."

Scripture Reading: Psalm 139:13-17

Key Verse: Psalm 139:14

I praise you because I am fearfully and wonderfully made; your works are wonderful, I know that full well.

———— ❖ ————

One evening our seven-year-old grandson Chad was helping Emilie set the dinner table. Whenever the grandchildren come over, Emilie honors someone at the table with our red plate that says, "You Are Special." When Emilie asked Chad, "Who should get the plate today?," we weren't surprised when he said, "How about me?"

After we sat down at the table and said the blessing, Chad spoke up: "I think it would be very nice if everyone around the table told me why they think I'm special." We got a chuckle out of that, but we also thought it was a good idea. After each of us told Chad why we thought he was special, Chad said, "Now I want to tell you why I think I'm special. I'm special because I'm a child of God."

Chad was absolutely right. Psalm 139:13-14 tells us that God knew each of us before we were born. He knit us together in our mother's womb and we are "wonderfully made." But unlike Chad, when I was seven—or 10 or even 22—I could not have told anyone why I was special. But one day when I read Psalm 139, I realized that I'm valuable

230

because I am a child of God, whom He knit together in my mother's womb.

Verse 16 of this psalm says, "All the days are ordained for me." It's not by accident that you are reading this selection today. God wants you to know how valuable you are. He has given you unique qualities, talents, and gifts. You are God's child, created by Him. He loves you more than any earthly father could, and He cares for you even when you feel worthless and far away. His love for you, His one-of-a-kind child, will never fail.

Father God, thank You for making me the person I am and for putting within me a heart to love You more and more each day. Help me today to draw nearer to You. And, as I go about my day, I can know that I am never alone. Thank You for always being with me. Amen.

Taking Action

❖ Thank God for who you are, His special child.

❖ Today, honor someone in your family for being special. A special plate isn't necessary. Be creative and come up with your own way of designating who's special.

❖ At an upcoming family meal, talk about why each person is special to the other family members and to God.

❖ Kidnap one of your children for lunch this week. Find out the exact time school breaks for lunch, notify the school office, and show up outside the classroom door. A nearby fast-food restaurant will do the trick and make your child feel special indeed.

❖

Reading On
Psalm 73:28   Ephesians 1:4

> Don't be afraid to take big steps. You
> can't cross a chasm in two small jumps.
>
> — *David Lloyd George*

Questions and Answers for Life

Scripture Reading: Romans 8:28-39

Key Verse: Romans 8:28

We know that in all things God works for the good of those who love him, who have been called according to his purpose.

———— ❖ ————

In today's Scripture passage, the apostle Paul asks and answers some key questions for life. Take a look at the powerful truth he outlines in Romans 8.

1. "What, then, shall we say in response to this?" (verse 31). Paul has written that God:

- Foreknew us.

- Predestined us to be conformed to the likeness of His Son.

- Called us.

- Justified us.

- Glorified us.

Then comes the question— "What, then, shall we say

in response to this?" Each one of us answers that question by how we live our life.

2. "If God is for us, who can be against us?" (verse 31)

Answer: Nothing— absolutely nothing on earth or in heaven above— can work against us because the Lord of the universe is for us. We have everything in God through His Son Jesus.

3. "He who did not spare his own Son, but gave him up for us all— how will he not also, along with him, graciously give us all things?" (verse 32)

Answer: God will graciously give us all the things that we need according to His will for our lives. What an assurance to know that what we have has passed through the Father's hands.

4. "Who will bring any charge against those whom God has chosen?" (verse 33)

Answer: No one— absolutely no one.

5. "Who is he that condemns?" (verse 34)

Answer: No one can condemn us because God, who is on our side, has justified us. Furthermore, Jesus Christ sits at the right hand of God interceding for us.

6. "Who shall separate us from the love of Christ?" (verse 35)

Answer: No one! And Paul gets specific. "Neither death nor life, neither angels nor demons, neither the present nor the future, nor any powers, neither height nor depth, nor anything else in all creation, will be able to separate us from the love of God that is in Christ Jesus our Lord" (verses 38-39).

Turn to these questions Paul asks and the answers he gives when the world crowds in and you're feeling alone. In His holy Word, God answers questions like the ones Paul asked as well as any questions you might ask—and Scripture's answers are the only reliable ones. So, during tough times, keep in mind that "in all things God works for the good of those who love him, who have been called according to his purpose" (verse 28).

> *Father God, when questions arise, guide me to the answers in Your Word. Give me discernment to ask the right questions in life and wisdom to discover Your answers. And thank You that, even when I blow it by asking the wrong questions or listening to the wrong answers, You can work my mistakes for my good. Amen.*

Taking Action

❖ What did you learn from today's Scripture that you didn't know before?

❖ What question for life do you want answered? Write it down and then go to Scripture. Also, don't hesitate to talk with a pastor, Bible study leader, or mature Christian for help in finding the answer.

Reading On
2 Timothy 3:16   1 John 1:5-2:2
Philippians 4:13

> A group of two hundred executives were asked what makes a person successful. Eighty percent listed enthusiasm as the most important quality.
>
> — *Unknown*

Key Promises of Scripture

Psalm 37:1-7

❖ *Evil men will fade away.*

❖ *Trust in the Lord and you will enjoy safe pasture.*

❖ *Delight in the Lord and He will give you your desires.*

❖ *Commit your way to the Lord and He will make your righteousness shine.*

Psalm 40:1-3

❖ *Wait patiently on the Lord and He will lift you out of the slimy pit, out of the mud and mire.*

❖ *He will set your feet on a firm rock.*

❖ *He will put a new song in your heart.*

Matthew 6:33

❖ *"Seek first his kingdom...and all of these things will be given to you.*

Romans 8:28-29

❖ *All things work together for good, to those who are loved and called according to His name.*

❖ *God knew us from the beginning of time.*

Romans 8:31

❖ *"If God is for us, who can be against us?"*

Romans 8:37-39

❖ *We are more than conquerors.*

❖ *Nothing can separate us from God's love.*

Philippians 1:6

❖ *"He who began a good work in you will carry it on to completion."*

Philippians 2:13

❖ *It is God who works in you for good.*

Philippians 4:4-8

❖ *"The peace of God...will guard your hearts and your minds in Christ Jesus."*

Philippians 4:13

❖ *"I can do everything through him who gives me strength."*

Philippians 4:19

❖ *"My God will meet all your needs according to his glorious riches in Christ Jesus."*

Bill McCartney
in **What Makes a Man**

Table Manners

Scripture Reading: Deuteronomy 6:1-9

Key Verses: Deuteronomy 6:6-7

> *These commandments that I give you today are to be upon your hearts. Impress them on your children. Talk about them when you sit at home and when you walk along the road, when you lie down and when you get up.*

Whatever happened to sitting down to the dinner table as a family— to good meals, no TV, and talk about what happened in each person's day? Does this sound foreign to you? Are you thinking, "Get real! We're living in the '90s. Life's not like it used to be"?

If you can't imagine regular family meals, think how startled the early Shaker settlers would be if they visited in our homes for an evening. To help you imagine their reaction, read through the following rules the Shakers have for children's behavior at the table.

Advice to Children on Behavior at the Table

First, in the morning, when you rise,
Give thanks to God, who well supplies
Our various wants, and gives us food,
Wholesome, nutritious, sweet, and good.

———— ❖ ————

Then to some proper place repair,
And wash your hands and face with care;
And ne'er the table once disgrace
With dirty hands or dirty face.
When to your meals you have the call,
Promptly attend, both great and small;
Then kneel and pray, with closed eyes,
That God will bless these rich supplies.
When at the table you sit down,
Sit straight and trim, nor laugh nor frown;
Then let the elder first begin,
And all unite, and follow him.
Of bread, then take a decent piece,
Nor splash about the fat and grease;
But cut your meat both neat and square,
And take of both an equal share.
Also, of bones you'll take your due,
For bones and meat together grew.
If, from some incapacity,
With fat your stomach don't agree,
Or if you cannot pick a bone,
You'll please to let them both alone.
Potatoes, cabbage, turnip, beet,
And every kind of thing you eat,
Must neatly on your plate be laid,
Before you eat with pliant blade;
Nor ever— 'tis an awkward matter,
To eat or sip out of the platter.
If bread and butter be your fare,
Or biscuit, and you find there are
Pieces enough, then take your slice,
And spread it over, thin and nice,
On one side, only; then you may

Eat in a decent, comely way.
Yet butter you must never spread
On nut-cake, pie, or dier-bread;
Or bread with milk, or bread with meat,
Butter with these you may not eat.
These things are all the best of food,
And need not butter to be good.
When bread or pie you cut or break,
Touch only what you mean to take;
And have no prints of fingers seen
On that that's left— nay, if they're clean.
Be careful, when you take a sip
Of liquid, don't extend your lip
So far that one may fairly think
That cup and all you mean to drink.
Then clean your knife— don't lick it, pray;
It is a nasty, shameful way—
But wipe it on a piece of bread,
Which snugly by your plate is laid.
Thus clean your knife, before you pass
It into plum or apple-sauce,
Or butter, which you must cut nice,
Both square and true as polish'd dice.
Cut not a pickle with a blade
Whose side with grease is overlaid;
And always take your equal share
Of coarse as well as luscious fare.
Don't pick your teeth, or ears, or nose,
Nor scratch your head, nor tonk your toes;
Nor belch nor sniff, nor jest nor pun,
Nor have the least of play or fun.
If you're oblig'd to cough or sneeze,
Your handkerchief you'll quickly seize,

And timely shun the foul disgrace
Of splattering either food or face.
Drink neither water, cider, beer,
With greasy lip or mucus tear;
Nor fill your mouth with food, and then
Drink, least you blow it out again.
And when you've finish'd your repast,
Clean plate, knife, fork—then, at the last,
Upon your plate lay knife and fork,
And pile your bones of beef and pork:
But if no plate, you may as well
Lay knife and fork both parallel.
Pick up your crumbs, and, where you eat,
Keep all things decent, clean, and neat;
Then rise, and kneel in thankfulness
To Him who does your portion bless;
Then straightly from the table walk,
Nor stop to handle things, nor talk.
If we mean never to offend,
To every gift we must attend,
Respecting meetings, work, or food,
And doing all things as we should.
Thus joy and comfort we shall find,
Love, quietness, and peace of mind;
Pure heavenly Union will increase,
And every evil work will cease.[37]

Quite a contrast to today's drive-through window at the local fast-food restaurant and kids, sitting in the back of a mini-van, eating with their fingers and licking the greasy sauce from the hamburger!

We've certainly come a long way from the Shakers' approach to dining—but we haven't gone in a good direction! Today's Scripture passage—like the poem above—challenges us to train our children. Instructions from the Lord are to be upon our hearts, we are to impress them upon our children, and talk about them when we walk along the road, when we lie down, and when we get up. What are you doing to properly train your children in all areas of life?

Father God, once again You've reminded me of the enormous privilege and responsibility of raising children. Give me energy, patience, creativity, and perseverance to train my children so that they will know You. Amen.

Taking Action

❖ Identify two or three areas of instruction for your children that you need to work on. What will you do to improve what you're doing for your children in each of these areas? What specific activities will help you strengthen a deficiency?

❖ Choose an evening to work on table manners. With your wife, plan an evening when the family can sit down together and enjoy a homemade meal. Depending upon your kids' ages, get them involved choosing the menu, cooking, serving, clearing the table, and coming up with questions that the whole family could talk about (how about "What's the best thing that happened to you today?"). As the leader of the family, don't leave the whole thing for your wife to do.

Reading On

Psalm 127:1-5	Proverbs 22:6
Proverbs 1:1-7	Luke 12:22-34

The Way Up

Scripture Reading: 1 Peter 5:5-11

Key Verse: 1 Peter 5:5b

> *All of you, clothe yourselves with humility toward one another, because, "God opposes the proud but gives grace to the humble."*

———— ❖ ————

Think about the last touchdown you saw scored. How did the player who carried the ball into the end zone react? Did he throw the ball to the ground as hard as he could? Do a jig? Give big bear hugs? Whatever he did, my guess is he didn't show much humility. And football players aren't the only ones short of humility. Baseball, basketball, and tennis players haven't mastered humility either, and that's not surprising in our world which has gone mad with pride.

I believe, however, that humility is key to successful relationships, but humility is a slippery characteristic. Once you think of yourself as humble— you're not! So people who are genuinely humble never perceive themselves as humble. Despite humility's slippery nature, the apostle Peter writes, "Clothe yourself with humility toward one another because God opposes the proud, but he gives grace to the humble. Humble yourselves, therefore, under God's mighty hand, that he may lift you up in due time" (1 Peter 5:5b-6).

Peter's words sharply contradict the message of today's

books on business, books that talk about climbing the corporate ladder, upward mobility, self-assertion, and winning through intimidation. The focus is always on moving up, but God's focus is different. The way up with God is always down. Peter's exhortation to be "clothed with humility" is a command, not a suggestion. And note that God opposes the proud. The moment we allow pride to raise its ugly head in our hearts, the resistance of God begins. We also learn in Isaiah that "the Lord detests all the proud" (Proverbs 16:5). And Proverbs 29:23 warns, "A man's pride brings him low."

Against that backdrop, hear the truth that Peter teaches: When you are clothed with humility, God ends His resistance against you. When we are humble, He promises to exalt us at the proper time:

- "Humility comes before honor" (Proverbs 15:33).

- "Humble yourself before the Lord, and He will lift you up" (James 4:10).

- "He has brought down rulers from their thrones but has lifted up the humble..." (Luke 1:52).

But what exactly is humility?

- It is moral realism, the result of a fresh revelation of God.

- It is esteeming others.

- It is a fruit of repentance.

- It is the attitude which rejoices in the success of others.

- It is freedom from having to be right.

- It is a foundation of unity.

- It is a mark of authenticity.

- It is a fruit of brokenness.

- It is a quality which catches the attention of God.

Our only response to God's holiness is humility, and the end result of our humility is holiness. As we kneel as servants at the foot of our Lord, ready and willing to serve Him and His people, He will lift us up.

> *Father God, give me such a clear vision of You, in all Your majesty and holiness, that I am humbled. Please make me aware of any false pride in my life. Send me a friend who can help me be accountable in this area of my life. And may the humility that comes from truly knowing You characterize all that I say and do. Amen.*

Taking Action

❖ List three or four areas of your life (business, athletics, cars, income, talents, etc.) which tend to make you prideful. Beside each item, write what you plan to do to find humility.

❖ Why do you think pride ruins relationships? Jot down a few thoughts.

Reading On
Proverbs 22:4   Philippians 2:8
Psalm 45:3-4   1 Peter 2:21

The Master Potter

Scripture Reading: Jeremiah 18:2-6

Key Verse: Jeremiah 18:6

> *"O house of Israel, can I not do with you as this potter does?"*

When our son Brad was in elementary school, the teacher asked the class to shape clay into something. Molded and shaped with his small hands, this red dinosaur-type thing that Brad proudly brought home is still on our bookshelf today.

Later, in high school, Brad enrolled in a ceramics class. His first pieces were crooked and misshaped, but as time went on he made some pieces of real art—vases, pots, pitchers, and various other kinds of pottery. Many pieces of clay he threw on the wheel, however, would take a different direction than he'd intended. Brad would work and work to reshape the clay, and sometimes he would have to start all over, working and working to make it exactly the way he wanted it to be.

With each one of us, God has, so to speak, taken a handful of clay to make us exactly who He wants us to be. He is the Master Potter, and we are the vessels in His house. As He shapes us on the potter's wheel, He works on the inside and the outside. He says, "I am with you. I am the Lord of your life and I will build within you a strong foundation based upon the Word of God."

The Master Potter also uses the circumstances of life to shape us into who He wants us to be. But when a child dies, the job loss occurs, fire destroys our home, finances dissolve, our marriage falls apart, or the children rebel, the Potter can seem very far away. We can feel forgotten by God, and we can pull away from Him who let us down. As time passes, He seems even more distant, and it seems that the Potter's work is put on hold. But God is the One who said, "I will never leave you nor forsake you."

When we feel far from God, we need to remember that God didn't put us on the shelf. We are the ones who moved away. He's ready to continue working to mold us into the person He intends us to be.

We also need to remember that, in pottery, the hot temperatures set the clay so the vessel doesn't leak and that the true beauty of the clay comes out only after the firing. The fires of life can do the same for our faith and our character, and we can rest in the knowledge that the Master Potter is at work.

> *Father God, You know I feel distant from You, but I know that I'm the one who moved. I've been trying to be the captain of my ship, but it's not working. I want to get back with Your program. I want You to shape me into the person You have designed me to be, and I want to work with You. I want to be malleable in Your hands. Amen.*

Taking Action

❖ When have you withdrawn from God and/or felt forgotten by Him? What circumstances prompted these feelings?

❖ What will you do to become more aware of the Master Potter— His love for you, His plan for you, and His ongoing work in your life?

Reading On

Psalm 73:26   Hebrews 13:5
Psalm 121:7   Romans 12:2

> Those who love Thy law have great peace, and nothing causes them to stumble.
>
> — *Psalm 119:165* NASB

In His Image

Everyone who comes to know Jesus stumbles because of him. He fails to meet our wrong expectations. He calls us to do impossible things or to become something we think we could never become. This is his way of teaching us how much we need him. He breaks us to pieces so that he can put us back together in his image.

— *Michael Card*

Using Your Talents

Scripture Reading: Matthew 25:14-30

Key Verse: Matthew 25:21

Well done, good and faithful servant!

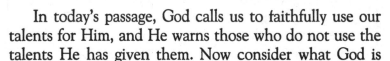

In today's passage, God calls us to faithfully use our talents for Him, and He warns those who do not use the talents He has given them. Now consider what God is saying specifically to you in this parable Jesus told.

What talents has God given you? Too often we think of talents as fully developed abilities, but it is only as we cultivate our talents that they become mature. Furthermore, we must be willing to take the risk of using our talents. When we do, we then find out how far God can take us.

Let's look at the story. In today's parable, the first two servants were willing to take a risk. Not only did they receive a 100-percent return for their efforts, but their master said, "Well done, good and faithful servant! You have been faithful with a few things: I will put you in charge of many things. Come and share your master's happiness!" (verses 21 and 23). Note that, despite their different talents and abilities, the first two servants received the same reward, indicating that God requires us to be faithful in the use of our abilities, whatever they are.

If you want to be successful in God's eyes, you must first

be faithful with a few things. Then God will put you in charge of many things. Is there a talent that people keep telling you you are good at, but you just shrug it off as not being good enough? Do you think no one could be blessed by your talent? This passage tells you to take the risk. Volunteer for that position, write that book, sign up for that class, offer to help with that project. Listen to God today as He calls you to the life of adventure that comes with using the gifts He's given you. Don't limit God.

Now let's look at the warning to those of us who don't use our talents. The third servant was afraid. Unwilling to take a risk with his one talent, he went and buried it in the ground. Are you burying your talents? God will hold you responsible for what you do with your talents, with your life. This third servant is condemned for his sloth and indifference.

God wants you to take the risk of using the talents He has given you, even if they don't seem like much to you. Take the first step today and you'll be amazed at what God can do with ordinary people. And you'll also be blessed when one day you stand before God and hear Him say, "Well done, good and faithful servant!"

> *Father God, at times I don't feel I have any talents, but I know You have given each of Your children special gifts. Today I'm asking You for direction. Lord, how do You want me to use my talents for Your glory? Thank You for listening to my prayer. Help me hear Your answer. Amen.*

Taking Action

❖ Ask God today to reveal to you those special gifts that He wants you to develop.

❖ Ask a friend to share with you his perception of your special gifts or talents.

❖ Develop a plan and a timetable to begin using these talents and gifts for the Lord.

Reading On
Exodus 4:10-12   Ephesians 3:14-21

> Teach us to number our days aright, that we may gain a heart of wisdom.
>
> — *Psalm 90:12*

Stewardship at Home

Scripture Reading: Psalm 127:1-128:4
Key Verse: Psalm 127:3
> *Sons are a heritage from the Lord, children a reward from him.*

In a recent Bible study Emilie attended, the teacher asked the women, "Did you feel loved by your parents when you were a child?" The answers were disturbing and, for us parents, quite convicting.

- "They were too busy for me."
- "I spent too much time with the babysitters."
- "Dad took us on trips, but he played golf all the time we were away."
- "I got in their way. I wasn't important to them."
- "Mom was too involved at the country club to spend time with us."
- "Mom didn't have to work, but she did so she wouldn't have to be home with us children."
- "A lot of pizzas were delivered to our house on Friday nights when my parents went out for the evening."

What do you think your children would say if someone asked them, "Do you feel loved by your parents?" Which of your actions would support their answer, positive or negative?

Today's Scripture reading gives us some principles for building a family in which children are confident that their parents love them. First, the psalmist addresses the foundation and protection of the home: "Unless the Lord builds the house, its builders labor in vain. Unless the Lord watches over the city, the watchmen stand guard in vain" (verse 1). The protective wall surrounding a city was the very first thing to be constructed when a new city was built. The people of the Old Testament knew they needed protection from the enemy, but they were also smart enough to know that walls could be climbed over, knocked down, or broken apart. They realized that their ultimate security was the Lord standing guard over the city.

Are you looking to God to help you build your home? Are you trusting the Lord to be the guard over your family? Many forces in today's society threaten the family. When I drive the Southern California freeways, I see parents who are burning the candle at both ends to provide for all the material things they think will make their families happy. We rise early and retire late. Psalm 127:2 tells us that these efforts are futile. We are to do our best to provide for and protect our family, but we must trust first and foremost in God to take care of them.

Then, in verse 3, we read that "children are a reward [gift] from [the Lord]." In the Hebrew, "gift" means "property," "possession." Truly, God has loaned us our children to care for and to enjoy for a certain period of time. They remain His property, His possessions. As stewards of our children, we are to take care of them, and that takes time.

I love to grow vegetables each summer, and I'm always amazed at what it takes to get a good crop. I have to cultivate the soil, sow the seeds, water, fertilize, weed, and prune. Raising children takes a lot of time, care, nurturing, and cultivating too. We can't neglect these responsibilities if we are going to produce good fruit. Left to themselves, our children—like the garden—will fall to seed and grow, if anything, only weeds. When I do tend the garden, however, I'm rewarded by corn, tomatoes, cucumbers, and beans. Just as the harvest is my reward, so God-fearing children are a parent's reward.

Next, comparing children to arrows in the hands of a warrior, Psalm 127:4-5 talks about how parents are to handle their offspring. Wise and skillful parents will know their children, understand them, and carefully point them in the right direction before shooting them into the world. And, as I learned in a college archery class, shooting an arrow straight and hitting a target is a lot harder in real life than it looks like in the movies or on TV. (I sure wasn't Robin Hood!) Likewise, godly and skillful parenting isn't easy.

The last section of today's selection teaches the importance of the Lord's presence in the home.

- The Lord is central to a home's happiness (128:1-2).

- A wife who knows the Lord will be a source of beauty and life in the home (128:3a).

- With the Lord's blessing, children will flourish like olive trees, which generously provide food, oil, and shelter for others (128:3b).

What can you do to make the Lord's presence more recognizable in your home?

Finally, to ask a more pointed question, what kind of steward are you being in your home? God has entrusted to you some very special people—your children. You will be held accountable for how you take care of them. But you're not in it alone. God offers guidelines like those we looked at today plus His wisdom and His love to help you do the job and do it well.

> *Father God, forgive me for the ways I short-
> change my kids. Help me know how to slow down
> the pace of life. Help me stay very aware that my
> children will only be with me for just a short time
> and that how I treat them will affect them and their
> children's lives, too. Continue to teach me how to be
> the father You want me to be. Amen.*

Taking Action

❖ "Our attitude toward our children reveals our attitude toward God." What does this statement mean to you?

❖ When you're talking to your children today, make a point of looking right into their eyes as you listen.

❖ Where do you need to be more consistent in teaching your children what is right and what is wrong?

❖ Give your child the gift of time—today and every day.

❖ Have you ever camped out inside? This weekend, go camping in your family room. Get your sleeping bags and a flashlight. Make shadow animals on the walls and ceilings. Review your week and plan something for the future. And don't forget the popcorn and hot chocolate.

Reading On

James 1:19-20   Proverbs 18:10
Matthew 18:5-6   Proverbs 16:24

> Do not call to mind the former things, or ponder things of the past. Behold, I will do something new.
>
> — *Isaiah 43:18-19*

A Treasure in Jars of Clay

Scripture Reading: 2 Corinthians 4:7; 6:3-10

Key Verse: 2 Corinthians 4:7

But we have this treasure in jars of clay to show that this all-surpassing power is from God and not from us.

———— ❖ ————

When our son Brad was in high school, he enjoyed ceramics. He was really quite good, and we still have many of his vases, jars, and pots. I was always amazed that Brad was able to make something beautiful out of a lump of reddish clay. When he added color and a glaze, it became a masterpiece.

In today's Scripture, we read that we are "jars of clay" and that we hold the great treasure of the gospel within. Isn't it interesting that you and I hide our treasures in vaults and safe deposit boxes, but God trusts His treasure to a common clay pot? The only value our clay pot has is in the treasure inside.

I am continually amazed that God can and does use me, an ordinary person who is willing to be used for Christ's sake. Simply stated, Christianity is Jesus Christ, the treasure, residing in the Christian, a clay pot. And God trusts us—even commands us—to share that treasure with other people.

Do you honestly believe that God can use you, a clay pot with a great treasure inside, to do the work He has called you to do for His kingdom? If we men could believe and act on this promise, God's kingdom would reign more fully in our hearts, our homes, our churches, our cities, our country, and the world.

> *Father God, don't let me hide my treasure—the knowledge of Your Son and my Savior Jesus Christ—in this clay pot. I want others around me to see what a precious and valuable treasure I, by Your grace, possess. And, Lord, I am only a clay pot, but in Your hands and strengthened by Your all-surpassing pow- er, You can use me for Your kingdom. I pray that You will do so. Amen.*

Taking Action

❖ What current problems make you feel like a clay pot?

❖ Where in your life do you think God wants to use you for His kingdom?

❖ Make these two lists the focus of your prayers. Know that God will give you the strength you need to deal with life's challenges. Know, too, that He wants to use you for His kingdom. As you pray, be ready to watch Him work in your life.

Reading On

Matthew 10:28-29   Philippians 4:13

Your Wife, Your Friend

Scripture Reading: Genesis 2:18-23

Key Verse: Genesis 2:18

> *The Lord God said, "It is not good for the man to be alone. I will make a helper, suitable for him."*

———— ❖ ————

In Genesis 2:18-23, we see that, when God created the first woman and wife, He also created the first friend. A wife is indeed to be her husband's friend, and Emilie has certainly been mine. And, as today's passage shows, that's what God intends for a married couple. Let's look closely at the Scripture.

- God gives the woman to the man to be "a helper suitable for him" (2:18)—How is your wife your helper? How does she help your work? Your time at home? Does she seem to often know what you need or want before you ask? How often do you let her know that you appreciate her helpfulness?

- God creates woman from man's rib (2:21-22)— In Genesis 1:27, we learn that God created human beings in His image. The fact that each of us is created in God's image calls us to honor and respect one another. What do you do to show your wife that you honor and respect her? How do you show and tell your wife that you love her?

- Adam perceived Eve as part of his own bone and own flesh (2:23)—If I recognize that Emilie is actually part of me, I will want to treat her as well as I treat myself. I will want to take good care of her and provide for her every need. What selfish behavior do you need to apologize for and change? What could you do to take better care of your wife?

In light of what you've seen in Scripture, consider the following definition of a friend:

> And what is a friend? Many things.... A friend is someone you are comfortable with, someone whose company you prefer. A friend is someone you can count on—not only for support, but for honesty.
> A friend is one who believes in you...someone with whom you can share your dreams. In fact, a real friend is a person you want to share all of life with—and the sharing doubles the fun.
> When you are hurting and you can share your struggle with a friend, it eases the pain. A friend offers you safety and trust.... Whatever you say will never be used against you.
> A friend will laugh with you, but not at you.... A friend will pray with you...and for you.
> My friend is one who hears my cry of pain, who senses my struggle, who shares my lows as well as my highs.[38]

In such a friendship, nothing is hidden. Such friendship is built on trust, and such friendship takes time to grow and develop. What better context for this kind of friendship to grow than your marriage? How does your marriage measure up?

> *Father God, I want to be a friend to my wife. Help me understand her better so that I can know how to support, encourage, and love her. Give me patience and a humble spirit that will serve, forgive, and ask forgiveness. Amen.*

Taking Action

❖ Do something with your wife that you don't normally like to do — watch a romantic movie, take her shopping, or plan a special dinner.

❖ Buy your wife a card or write her a note telling how much you enjoy her as a friend.

Reading On

Proverbs 18:24   Amos 3:3   Ecclesiastes 4:9

Let no unwholesome word proceed from your mouth, but only such a word as is good for edification...that it may give grace to those who hear.

— *Ephesians 4:29* NASB

The Guy Who
Drew the Line

Scripture Reading: Ephesians 1:3-14

Key Verse: Ephesians 1:4

For he chose us in him before the creation of the world to be holy and blameless in his sight.

———— ❖ ————

The judge looked down from the bench and, in a somber voice, declared, "Mr. Wilson, this is your day of reckoning!" Then he sentenced him to seven and one-half years in federal prison.

In response, Wilson's lawyer requested that he be allowed a few minutes with his family and friends before surrendering to the authorities.

The judge replied, "Mr. Wilson is going to be taken by the marshals right now. You should have thought of that before."

Wilson was one of four California men convicted of financial fraud and sentenced to prison in this particular case. Five men were originally investigated, but the fifth, Mark Jacobs, was not arrested and charged.

Jacobs had been invited to join the financial scheme by four friends (the men sent to jail) in a weekly Bible study. They had assured him their plan was totally legal. Yet something inside him said it wasn't right. While it was hard to say no to good friends, he chose to go with his conscience and tell them he wouldn't participate.

The lawyers for the four convicted men pleaded with the judge that their clients had simply made mistakes of poor judgment. They were good men who loved their wives and kids, gave to charities, and were active in their churches. The crime involved a "gray" area, crossing a line that wasn't clear.

The judge disagreed. "It is not hard to determine where the line is," he said. "The guy who drew the line is Mark Jacobs. He knew what was right and what was wrong, and he didn't hesitate. Hopefully, now we will have fewer people who are willing to walk up to the line and dabble with going over the line. We will have people like Mr. Jacobs, who wouldn't touch this thing with a ten-foot pole." [39]

Too often in America today, men in responsible positions don't know where to draw the line. We see it in the worlds of high finance, religion, politics, entertainment, and sports. Our ethics and morality are no longer firmly anchored in the Judeo-Christian principles of our forefathers. Without these guidelines to show us where to draw the line, we are confused and adrift when it comes to knowing right and wrong, and we aren't able to live the kind of life Christ calls us to live.

In 1 Peter 1:6-7, we are reminded that we become pure just as gold does. It's a process. As one writer explains,

"Gold has to be heated and reheated and reheated several times for the alloys and impurities to be brought to the surface, where the goldsmith can remove them. If you forget that becoming pure is a process, you risk becoming overwhelmed by discouragement when you experience those inevitable setbacks."[40]

Wanting to be pure in a world of gray isn't enough. You have to develop a plan of action if you are to become more like Jesus. In *Seven Promises of a Promise Keeper*, Dr. Gary Oliver lists some simple steps you and I can take so that God can move us beyond good intentions and down the path toward purity:

1. Make a decision (Daniel 1:8).
2. Choose to put first things first (Mark 7:15, 20-23).
3. Determine where the line is and then stay a safe distance behind it (James 1:14-15).
4. Guard your heart (Matthew 6:21).
5. Guard your mind (Colossians 3:2).
6. Guard your eyes (Job 31:1).
7. Guard the little things (Luke 16:10).[41]

These steps are simply stated, but not necessarily easy to live out. I challenge you to try. Ask God to strengthen your commitment to Him and to guide your thoughts as you turn to Him to learn how to be a godly and pure man, a man who knows where to draw the line in our confusing world.

Father God, I come before You concerned about how I can live a pure life. I want to make right decisions. I want to live a life that reflects to my family and to the world that I am a child of Your kingdom. When I need to make choices in this confusing world but don't know where Your line is, please take a stick and draw that line for me. Give me a daily hunger for Your Word that I may learn and live according to the black and white You teach there. Then help me be a guy who draws the line. Amen.

Taking Action

❖ Develop a specific plan, based on the seven steps outlined above, that will help you live a purer, more Christlike life.

❖ Begin reading your Bible daily. Start with the Gospel of John, the Psalms, or Proverbs. As you read, ask yourself what God is showing you about how to live a pure life.

❖ Find a friend who will hold you accountable to your plan or, better yet, join you in your study.

Reading On

Matthew 5:8   Ephesians 4:1   Ephesians 5:1

Do not withhold your mercy from me, O LORD; may your love and your truth always protect me.

— *Psalm 40:11*

For the Traveling Man

❖ Decide beforehand not to indulge in pornography. Most mistakes are made when you haven't resolved to avoid the material before you leave home.

❖ Whenever possible, stay with friends when you're traveling alone. If you're around others, you're less likely to give in to temptations.

❖ When you check in at a hotel, request that the staff block the adult movies from your room. If you do, you'll face much less temptation later in the evening.

❖ Develop a game plan for your evening. Outline the specific things you want to see and do before settling in for the night. If you fill your time with productive uses, you'll be less tempted.

❖ Make a habit of reading Scripture before turning on the TV. Try Psalm 101:2-4, Romans 12:21, 1 Corinthians 6:18-20, Ephesians 6:10-17; James 4:17.

— Based on Jerry Kirk
in **Seven Promises of a Promise Keeper**

Asking "Why?"

Scripture Reading: Ecclesiastes 7:13-18

Key Verse: Ecclesiastes 7:16

*Do not be overrighteous, neither be overwise—
why destroy yourself?*

———— ❖ ————

You have to know that fame is fleeting, and I know— I always had my parents to refresh my memory.

No matter how important you think you are, they taught me, you're a mere nothing in the passage of time. Once you reach a certain level in a material way, what more can you do? You can't eat more than three meals a day; you'll kill yourself. You can't wear two suits, one over the other. You might now have three cars in your garage— but six! Oh, you can indulge yourself, but only to a point.

One way to make sure fame doesn't change you is to keep in mind that you're allotted only so much time on this earth— and neither money nor celebrity will buy you a couple of extra days. Although I do have a rich friend in New York who says, "What do you mean I can't take it with me? I've already made out traveler's checks and sent them ahead."

Life is so complicated that it's hard for anyone, especially kids, to figure out what their purpose is in life, and to whom they're account-able. Of course, we should all be accountable to God throughout our lives— and live our lives that way every day, not just on our deathbeds begging for forgiveness.

A lot of people don't believe in God because they can't see him. I'm not a Doubting Thomas, though. I truly believe. When we were kids, our Sunday School teachers used to address this question by telling us: "You can't see electricity either, but it's there. Just stick your hand in the socket now and then to remind yourself." I've never seen an ozone layer or carbon monoxide or an AIDS virus, but they're out there some-where.[42]

Lee Iacocca has a realistic and balanced perspective on wealth and fame. He knows that earthly things will pass away and that he's ultimately accountable to God. Are you and I living in light of these truths?

In today's Scripture, we see that God brings both prosperity and adversity into our lives for His sovereign purpose but without always revealing His plan. Our minds do not have the horsepower to think as God does. That means we must, by faith, rely on His promises and trust that He will do what He says He will do. We learn, however, in 2 Timothy 3:16-17 that "all Scripture is God-breathed and is useful for teaching, rebuking, correcting and training in righteousness, so that the man of God may be thoroughly equipped for every good work."

Are you letting God's Word help equip you to handle

life—to deal with birth, death, fame, fortune, bankruptcy, wealth or poverty, health or sickness? Are you letting God's Word help equip you for the times you ask, "Why?" about something that happens and are unable to even begin to answer that question? "Why?" is the mystery question of life. Solomon, the writer of Ecclesiastes, realized that God has a sovereign purpose but that He doesn't always explain it to us.

As I work on this devotion, I can't help thinking about a recent funeral. Chuck White, a prominent businessman, attorney, and Christian leader in the community, was 52 years old when, while pitching for his church's softball team, he collapsed and died instantly of a massive heart attack. God was using Chuck in the community, at the local high school, in the business world, and in his family. Why did God take this man so soon? We don't know the answer to that question. So we remind ourselves that we belong to a God who is loving and just, whose timing is perfect and ways are right. We walk by faith and not by sight and let the "Why?" go unanswered this side of heaven.

> *Father God, humble me so I might be open to Your truths and so I can let go of the need to know "Why?" Help me to let You be God and to accept that I can't understand Your ways. At those times, help me to trust in Your love, Your mercy, and Your goodness. Amen.*

Taking Action

❖ List several of your "why" questions, realizing that you will not know all the answers.

❖ Turn your "why" questions over to God in prayer and

give them up to Him. Someday you will realize how these whys fit into His sovereign plans.

❖ Thank God, also, for all the questions you have answers for.

Reading On
Ecclesiastes 3:1-8   Ecclesiastes 3:14
Ecclesiastes 9:1

The quality of a person's life is in direct proportion to their commitment to excellence, regardless of their chosen field of endeavor.

— *Vince Lombardi*

A House Divided

Scripture Reading: Mark 3:24-27

Key Verse: Mark 3:25

If a house is divided against itself, that house cannot stand.

———— ❖ ————

"A house divided against itself cannot stand," Abraham Lincoln said when he accepted the nomination for a United States Senate seat. "Either the opponents of slavery will arrest the further spread of it and place it where the public mind shall rest in the belief that it is in the course of ultimate extinction, or its advocates will push it forward, till it shall become alike lawful in all the states, old as well as new—north as well as south."

Lincoln's stand against slavery and for the equality of peoples resulted in his defeat in the election, but Lincoln responded philosophically: "Though I now sink out of view and shall be forgotten, I believe I have made some marks which will tell for the cause of civil liberty long after I am gone." Well, Lincoln certainly didn't "sink out of view"! As President of the United States, he worked to bring together those who had been at war and to heal the hurts that had divided the nation and even some families within it.

Many families today are divided and need to be brought together; many hurts in those families need to be healed. I've watched this happen in Emilie's family. Her two aunts were sisters who hadn't spoken to each other for 10 years. The initial disagreement, as slight as it may have been, became unbridgeable. Neither would apologize or admit to being wrong. Having watched this go on for a long time, Emilie decided that she was going to be the peacemaker. She arranged a family gathering and invited both aunts. After just a short time, the two began to open up and talk to each other. By the end of the evening, they had made amends, and they were able to enjoy the last 15 years of their lives together.

Maybe such division exists in your family. If so, know that the warning in today's Scripture is for you—"If a kingdom is divided against itself, that kingdom cannot stand." If a family remains divided, it will collapse. What can you do to help bring unity to your family? What can you do to help healing come to your home? Whatever steps you decide to take, know that you'll need much patience and many prayers. As you seek God's blessing on your attempts to rebuild your home, ask Him to give you wisdom and understanding. Know, too, that it will take time to rebuild what has been destroyed by division; don't feel that it must be resolved quickly. Be willing to walk by faith, not by sight, and pray earnestly for healing each step of the way.

Father God, use me to be a healer in my family. Use me to help bring unity where there is now division. Show me the steps to take. I thank You that You will be with me and my family members as we try to build bridges and learn to forgive one another. Amen.

Taking Action

❖ Where in your family is there division? Where is there a need for healing and reunification? What one person could you start focusing your prayers on?

❖ Ask your wife to join you in praying about this person and the goal of unity within the family.

❖ Develop a plan for reuniting this family member with the family and then take the risky step of putting that plan into action.

Reading On

Matthew 12:25-27   Luke 11:17-22

For I am confident of this very thing, that He who began a good work in you will perfect it until the day of Christ Jesus.

— *Philippians 1:6*

Worthy of Love

Scripture Reading: Matthew 22:36-40

Key Verses: Matthew 22:37-39

> *"Love the Lord your God with all your heart and with all your soul and with all your mind." This is the first and greatest commandment. And the second is like it: "Love your neighbor as yourself."*

In Matthew 22, Jesus quotes from Deuteronomy 6:4-9, words which became part of Judaism's basic confession of faith. According to rabbinic law, this Old Testament passage—which stresses the uniqueness of God, precludes the worship of other gods, and demands the people's total commitment—was to be recited every morning and night.

Now, thousands of years later, Jesus is asked, "Teacher, which is the greatest commandment in the Law?" Jesus reduced the entire Law to two commandments which call us to love God, love our neighbor, and love our self. We know we ought to love God and love our neighbors, but what does it mean for us men to love ourselves?

Challenged by this question, I studied what the Bible says about personal worth, and I looked at the men around me. I saw many who struggled to accept themselves, whose lives reflected fear, guilt, and mistrust of other people. These men did not understand that their Creator God had given them certain divine dignity which could make it possible for them to love themselves and realize they are worthy of love.

I also noticed that men's relationships with their wives, their children, and their friends were positive or negative depending how well they understood that they were loved by God. People who cannot love themselves do not dare love other people. Their fears are too great. They are afraid they'll be rejected. Why do they have that fear? Because they do not believe they'll be loved, and rejection would further confirm for them that they aren't worthy of love. Such negative voices speak loudly. But hear now God's truth.

Genesis 1:26-27 says, "Then God said, 'Let us make man in our image, in our likeness...' So God created man in his own image, in the image of God he created him; male and female he created them." Verse 31 reads, "God saw all that he had made [and that means you!], and it was very good." Recognizing God's evaluation of us, the human beings He created, helps us realize that we are worthy of love— of godly self-love as well as the love of others.

When George Gallup, Jr., conducted a poll on the self-esteem of the American public, the poll revealed that people with a positive self-image demonstrate the following qualities:

1. They have a high moral and ethical sensitivity.
2. They have a strong sense of family.

3. They are far more successful in interpersonal relationships.
4. Their perspective on success is viewed in terms of interpersonal relationships, not in crass materialistic terms.
5. They're far more productive on the job.
6. They are far lower in incidents of chemical addictions. (Current research shows that 80 percent of all suicides are related to alcohol and drug addiction.)
7. They are more likely to get involved in social and political activities in their community.
8. They are far more generous to charitable institutions and give far more generously to relief causes.[43]

As contributing members of our family, church, community, and society, each of us wants these positive qualities, and those qualities come when we trust that we are valuable people, created by God. When we view God as a personal, loving, and forgiving Father and relate to Him in such a personal way, we can develop a strong, healthy sense of self-worth. And such self-love is not evil and wrong. It's good stewardship of the unique person God created you to be.

Father God, I don't want to become self-centered, but I do want to understand the value You have given me because You created me and You sent Your Son to die for me. Please help me to accept, with Your love, those parts of myself that I find difficult to love. Begin transforming those qualities that I may become more like Christ. And throughout this process, help me base my sense of self-worth on You and You alone. Amen.

Taking Action

❖ Write down five things you like about yourself.

❖ Now write down five things you want to improve about yourself.

❖ After each item on the second list, write one or two things you are going to do to improve that area of your life.

❖ Take time to read through Psalm 139 and consider what those truths say about your value.

Reading On

Deuteronomy 6:4-9   Philippians 4:13
Genesis 1:26-27

What Do Women Do All Day?

Scripture Reading: Proverbs 31:10-31
Key Verses: Proverbs 31:10-11

> *A wife of noble character who can find? She is worth far more than rubies. Her husband has full confidence in her and lacks nothing of value.*

Every minute, to and fro, that's the way my
    hours go;
Bring me this, and take me that, feed the dog,
    and take out the cat.

Standing up, I eat my toast, drink my coffee,
    thaw the roast,
Empty garbage, make the bed, rush to church,
    then wash my head.

Sweep the kitchen, wax the floor, scrub the
    woodwork, clean the doors;
Scour the bathtub, then myself. Vacuum
    carpets, straighten shelves.

Eat my sandwich on the run...now my
    afternoon's begun.

❖

To the baseball game I go, when will there be
    time to sew?
Meet the teacher, stop the fight, see the
    dentist, fly the kite.
Help with homework, do the wash, iron the
    clothes, put on the squash.

Shop for groceries, cash a check, fight the
    crowds, now I'm a wreck!
Dinner time it soon will be. "What's for
    supper?" Wait and see!

Dirty dishes crowd the sink, next there's
    popcorn, then a drink.
Will they never go to bed? Will I ever get
    ahead?

"Bring me water," "Get the light." Turn off
    TV, lock the bike.
"Where's my pillow?" "Hear my prayers." "Did
    you lock the door downstairs?"

At last in bed, my spouse and I, too tired to
    move, too weak to cry.
But e'er I doze, I hear him say, "WHAT DO
    WOMEN DO ALL DAY?" [44]

Do you ever wonder what your wife is doing all day while you're at work? If you're the chief or only breadwinner, you might think, "What my wife does is important— but it's not like what I do!" But the poem above— and simply looking around your own home— can open your eyes to the demands of home and family management.

———— ❖ ————

As I've watched my wife Emilie and many of her friends, I've been amazed at how much they get done— all at the same time. They seem able to juggle a lot more balls at one time than I can. You get more than two balls going for me and I am on overload. I am basically a "one baller." Emilie, on the other hand, can handle five balls well.

I remember when the children were younger and I was home for a few days— and I couldn't wait to get back to work. In fact, on several occasions I checked myself out of the house before the doctor gave me a release. Why? I couldn't handle all the balls going at one time.

If watching your wife in action doesn't give you reason enough to appreciate her, consider the standards God has for your wife. These are listed in today's passage:

- She is very valuable (verse 10).

- We are to have full confidence in her (verse 11).

- Our wife is to bring us good, not harm (verse 12).

- She is to be industrious (verse 13).

- She is to be a good cook, shopper, delegator, realtor, gardener, overseer, seamstress; she works long hours; she is to be compassionate and serene (verse 14-22).

- She is to bring respect and honor to us as her husband (verse 23).

- She is to have a good sense of humor, be wise with her words, and not be lazy (verse 24-27).

- She is to be respected and praised by her children (verse 28).

- She is to be praised by her husband (verse 29).

- She has no comparison in all the world (verse 29).

- She is to major on the majors, not the minors (verse 30).

- She is to be rewarded and praised (verse 31).

That's a tall order for your wife and mine—but a wife who strives to meet these standards is a real helpmate to us. God knows what we need in order for us to function properly as a husband and the head of the family, and He tells us here. Our response to this gift of a godly and hard-working wife is to thank God and to appreciate her. Take time today to consider all that your wife does all day— and then let her know that you appreciate her.

> *Father God, thank You for reminding me today of all that my wife does for our family. Forgive me for the times I take her for granted and take for granted her contributions to our home. Teach me to encourage her and show her how much I appreciate her. She is definitely worthy of praise. Amen.*

Taking Action

❖ Include in a special "I love you"/ "thank you" card some fun confetti in the shapes of hearts, dogs, cats, stars, moons, etc.

❖ Take your wife shopping this evening and find her a new outfit.

❖ Be a genie: Grant your wife three wishes.

❖ Tell your wife that you are thankful for her because _____.

❖ You do, of course, have a picnic basket (full of food and drinks) in your car trunk at all times, don't you?

❖ Just thought you might like to know...the proper way to kiss a woman's hand is to hold her hand gently but firmly in a comfortable position. Lower your lips to her hand. Do not raise her hand to your lips.

Reading On

Proverbs 12:4   1 Peter 3:1-6

The woman is the glory of man.

— *1 Corinthians 11:7*

A Rat in a Maze

Scripture Reading: Galatians 5:7-10, 13-15

Key Verse: Galatians 5:7

You were running a good race. Who cut in on you and kept you from obeying the truth?

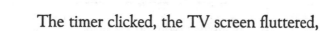

The timer clicked, the TV screen fluttered, and the speaker blared the morning news.

"Morning already?" groaned Larry. He rolled over and squeezed the pillow tightly over his ears, not seriously thinking he could muffle the announcement of another day in the rat race. Then the aroma of coffee from the timer-operated percolator lured him toward the kitchen.

Six hours of sleep may not have been the house rule growing up, but success at the end of the twentieth century demanded a premium from its active participants. A rising star like Larry couldn't squander time sleeping.

Curls of steam rose from the bowl of instant oatmeal; the microwave had produced predict-ably perfect results in perfect cadence with his thirty-five-minute wake-up schedule.

Slouched in his chair, propped against his elbow, Larry noticed the computer screen staring back at him. Last night he balanced his check-book after the eleven o'clock news, and, weary from the long day, he must have neglected to switch it off.

His wife, Carol, had welcomed a day off, so she slept in. Larry went through the rote motions of getting the kids off to school. After the two younger children had been dropped off at day-care, he was alone in the car with Julie. Twelve-year-old Julie seemed troubled lately. "Daddy, do you love mom anymore?" she asked. The question came out of the blue to Larry, but Julie had been building the courage to ask it for months. Their family life was changing, and Julie seemed to be the only member of the family diagnosing the changes. Larry reassured her he loved mom very much.

Carol didn't plan to go back to work when she first started on her MBA degree. Bored with her traditional, nonworking-housewife role, she just wanted more personal self-fulfillment. Her magazines conferred no dignity on the role of mother-tutor.

Although her family satisfied her self-esteem need for many years, other neighborhood women her same age seemed to lead glamorous lives in the business world. She couldn't help but question her traditional values.

"Maybe I'm too old-fashioned— out of step with the times," she thought to herself.

So, two nights each week for three and a half years she journeyed off to the local university, a big investment—not to mention the homework.

By the time she walked across the stage to receive her diploma, Carol was convinced women had a right to professional fulfillment just as much as men.

Larry, a tenacious, carefree sales representative, advanced quickly in his company. Fifteen years of dream chasing rewarded him with a vice-president's title. The pay covered the essentials, but they both wanted more of the good life.

"I've been thinking about going back to work," Carol told him.

Larry didn't protest. She earned extra money as a bank teller at the beginning of their marriage, and the money helped furnish their honeymoon apartment. By mutual agreement, Carol stopped working when Julie was born, and ever since they had been hard-pressed to make ends meet.

Even though his own mother didn't work, Larry knew things were different for women. Still, he had mixed emotions about sending their two small children to a day-care center. But since money was always a problem, he just shrugged and kept silent when Carol announced she had started interviewing for a job.

Larry clearly understood the trade-off. More money, less family. More family, less money. Yet, they really wanted the good life.

Their neighbors bought a twenty-four-foot cabin cruiser. Larry was surprised to learn they could own one, too, for only $328 per month. By scrimping for five months they pulled together $1,000 which, when added to their savings, gave them enough for the $2,500 down payment.

Larry loved cars. His gentle dad had always loved cars. If a shiny two-door pulled up to him at a traffic light, Larry's heart always beat faster—he could just picture himself shifting through the gears of a fancy European import. By accident he discovered that for only $423 a month he could lease the car of his fantasies—a racy import! Leasing never occurred to him before.

Carol desperately wanted to vacation in Hawaii that year; her Tuesday tennis partner went last spring. But they couldn't do both.

"If you go along with me on this one, I'll make it up to you, Carol. I promise!" Larry told her, his infectious grin spreading across his face. She reminisced how that impish little-boy smile had first attracted her to him. He had been good to her, she thought.

"Okay, go ahead," Carol told him.

His dad had always loved Chevys. Larry's tastes had evolved with the times.

Carol dreamed of living in a two-story home with a swimming pool, but, with the car and boat payments so high, it remained a dream for years. Larry slaved twelve- and fourteen-hour days, always thinking of ways to earn more money for Carol's dream house. When Carol went to work, they added up the numbers and were elated to see they could finally make the move.

The strain of keeping their household afloat discouraged them. There were bills to pay, kids to pick up from day-care, deadlines to meet, quotas to beat, but not much time to enjoy the possessions they had accumulated.

Words from a Simon and Garfunkel song haunted Larry's thoughts: "Like a rat in a maze, the path before me lies. And the pattern never alters, until the rat dies." He was trapped.

Carol pressured out—she just couldn't take it anymore. She believed Larry had let her down. He was supposed to be strong. He was supposed to know how to keep everything going. But Larry was just as confused about their situation as she was.

As the U-Haul van pulled away from the house Larry couldn't quite believe she was actually doing it— Carol was moving out. She said she just needed some time and space to sort things out, that she was confused. The question Julie had asked a few months earlier burned in his mind, "Daddy, do you love mom anymore?" Yes...yes, he loved her, but was it too late? How did things get so out of hand?[45]

I'm sure you know your fair share of Larrys. In fact, Larry may even remind you of yourself. If so, let this be a wake-up call. No one wins the rat race! No one!

Are you trying to win the rat race? If so, you might consider making some dramatic changes before one of your children asks you, "Daddy, do you love Mommy?" and you find you can't say, "Yes."

Why do we run in a race that has no winners?

Lord God, I want to run this race called life for You. But it's hard for me to know how to get out of the rat race I feel so caught up in. Give me clarity.

Help me develop proper priorities—Your priorities
for my life and for my family. Help me to be the man
You want me to be. Amen.

Taking Action

- Where do you see yourself in the story of Larry and Carol?

- How did you get caught up in the race that doesn't produce winners?

- What changes are you going to start making today?

Reading On

1 Corinthians 6:12   Ecclesiastes 5:10
Romans 12:1-2   2 Corinthians 5:17

Devote yourselves to prayer, keeping alert
in it with an attitude of thanksgiving.

— Colossians 4:2

Thriving on the Job

❖ *Strengthen relationships with co-workers.*
This may mean going to a fellow worker and asking, "What can I do to help us work better together?" Improved relationships will help you feel better about going to work.

❖ *Stay away from complainers.*
Surround yourself with positive, encouraging people.

❖ *Learn to delegate.*
Someone around you just might love to do those jobs you hate. Ask around!

❖ *Try to understand your boss.*
Since much of your stress will come from the person above you, spend time understanding his position. Let your boss know that you are a supporter and want to know him/her better.

❖ *Leave your job at lunch.*
Do something different to break your routine, relieve your stress, and stimulate your creativity.

❖ *Find a special project just for you.*
Talk to your supervisor about assigning you a special task. You'll find new excitement for work and have a chance to show your boss what you can do.

❖ *Learn new skills.*
Someone at work or a night class at the local college may be just the ticket to learning something new.

❖ *Give yourself away.*
Volunteer your skills to a non-profit organization.

❖ *Reward yourself.*
If you're having a bad day, reward yourself with a special treat for lunch or your favorite workout.

❖ *Remember that every job has its problems.*
Hang in there when you're discouraged. The grass isn't any greener elsewhere.

The Los Angeles Marathon

Scripture Reading: Hebrews 12:1-12

Key Verses: Hebrews 12:1-2

> *Therefore, since we are surrounded by such a great cloud of witnesses, let us throw off everything that hinders and the sin that so easily entangles, and let us run with perseverance the race marked out for us. Let us fix our eyes on Jesus, the author and perfecter of our faith, who for the joy set before him endured the cross, scorning its shame, and sat down at the right hand of the throne of God.*

Our son, Brad, has always been an athlete. Name the sport and he could do it—and do it well. In high school he played football. In college he played volleyball and tennis. After graduation he and some college friends began doing triathlons (swimming, biking, and running), and Brad did very well.

When Brad was 30, he met Maria, the ideal woman for him because she loved athletics, too. On their first date, they jogged through Central Park in New York City. Not long after they were married.

In the spring of 1991, Brad and Maria entered the Los Angeles Marathon. They both worked out hard and long

291

for the 26.2 mile run. Every day before or after work, they ran between 6 and 19 miles a day, enough to total 75 miles a week. Finally, the day of the marathon arrived. Brad and Maria had prepared well. At the sound of the gun, over 20,000 runners were off.

That day wasn't a good day for Brad. Although he had prepared for months and faithfully maintained a rigorous training schedule, he had hit the wall by the tenth mile. Physically, he was Mr. America, but that day he just wasn't able to perform. He continued to run, struggling painfully on. Brad finished the race—he's always finished whatever he starts—but his time was 3 hours and 50 minutes. His goal had been just a little over three hours.

Maria had an up day. She finished in 3 hours and 25 minutes. When she crossed the finish line, she immediately began looking for Brad, but she couldn't find him. She began to check the stretchers lined with runners who had fallen out of the race. No Brad. She grew concerned as she asked friends and others on the sidelines. No Brad! She was amazed later to find that Brad had come in after she had. It was an experience they will never forget.

As tough a day as it was for Brad, he helped me appreciate the truth of our text in Hebrews. In this race called life, we are to keep our eyes on Jesus and continue running toward the mark He has set for us. We must discipline ourselves to study God's Word and get to know Him better so that we can continue on even when we hit the wall. When we do, He begins to produce in our hearts a harvest of righteousness and peace. We become mature, strong, and able to help others through their struggles. And when we struggle and even fall along the way, we need to do what Brad did. Rather than looking back at a bad race and asking "Why?," he looks ahead to the day when he'll run it again.

The author of Hebrews tells us other things about this race of life:

- We are surrounded by other Christians and can get support from them.

- We need to throw off everything that hinders us.

- We need to throw off the sin that entangles us.

- We need to run with perseverance and determination.

- And we need to fix our eyes on Jesus, the Author and Perfecter of our faith.

With God's help, we will run this race and cross the finish line in His perfect time.

> *Father God, help me each day to run with perseverance the race of life so that I might bring glory to Your name. Teach me self-discipline and give me Your strength to go the distance. Amen.*

Taking Action

❖ List those areas of your life where you need to be more disciplined: physical health, mental health, organizational skills, eating, financial matters, family, business dealings, etc. What will you do to become more disciplined? Be specific.

❖ Are there any things from a past race that you are still holding onto? If so, give them to the Lord today. Then, with your eyes fixed on Jesus, keep running.

Reading On
Isaiah 40:31   1 Corinthians 9:24

> Most people are about as happy as they make up their minds to be.
>
> — *Abraham Lincoln*

Waiting on God

    To wait on God is to struggle and sometimes to fail. Sometimes the failures teach us more than the successes. For the failures teach us that to wait on God is not only to wait for his mercy, but to wait by his mercy.... The glory hidden in our failures is the discovery that the very thing we wait for is what we wait by! The success of our waiting lies not in who we are, but in who God is. It is not our strength that will pull us through to the end. It is God's amazing grace and mercy.

— Ben Patterson

What Happens When We Die?

Scripture Reading: Psalm 71:14-18

Key Verse: Psalm 71:18

Even when I am old and gray, do not forsake me, O God, till I declare your power to the next generation, your might to all who are to come.

———— ❖ ————

As I get older, I think more and more about what comes next. I know there's got to be something else after this life is over, because I can't grasp the alternative. I can't imagine that through all eternity I'll never see anyone I love again, that my whole awareness will just be obliterated. I can't believe that we are only bodies passing through.

When I muse about this, I think of all the great moments I had with my father. It's inconceivable that I had this wonderful period in life with him and then suddenly the curtain dropped. Instead, I want to believe I'm going to meet up with him again. I also want to have the opportunity to catch up with Mary, if only to tell her what I forgot to tell her, and to meet all my lifelong friends who have died. I do think they're out there someplace.

I haven't yet formed a clear idea about what the hereafter might be like. I don't know if everyone's an angel, or an apparition. Or it's just all beyond comprehension. But I do hope that it's going to be better than here, because life on this planet is not exactly peaches and cream. I mean, this life is tough. I suppose that's the promise religion holds out. If you can take this life as it comes and give it your best, there will be something better afterwards.

I've always marveled at how belief in the hereafter gets accentuated as people grow older. Until their deathbeds, many of the great minds in science thought that because their soul and being were wrapped up in their body— the old ninety-eight cents' worth of chemicals— and that because after death these would no longer be a body, that was it. But now when they have to go, suddenly they want to believe in somebody up there because they don't know where they're going and they are scared.[46]

These thoughts of Lee Iacocca touch on questions we all ask, and those can be boiled down to "What happens when we die?" Those of us who know the Lord have a better idea than the people around us who don't. And the psalmist who wrote today's Scripture understands the urgency of letting those folks know what we already know. The psalmist prays that God would not forsake him until he declares His power to the next generation. The psalmist knew he had work to do— and so do you and I.

In case you're not sure what that work is, read Jesus' command and promise in Matthew 28:19-20: "Therefore

———— ❖ ————

go and make disciples of all nations, baptizing them in the name of the father and of the Son and of the Holy Spirit, and teaching them to obey everything I have commanded you. And surely I am with you always, to the very end of the age."

We are commanded to share the news of sin and salvation. How well do you do that? Maybe it's hard for you to talk about your faith because you're unsure of the message. This following passages can help you brush up on the basics so you can be more confident as you talk about Jesus with those who don't know Him as their Lord and Savior.

- Romans 3:23

- Romans 6:23

- Acts 16:30-31

- Ephesians 2:8-9

- Romans 10:9-10

- John 10:28

- John 14:2-3

Once you've reviewed these truths, you can then invite the person you're sharing with to receive Christ by faith through a prayer like this one:

> *Lord Jesus, I need You. Thank You for dying on the cross for my sins. I open the door of my life and receive You as my Savior and Lord. Thank You for forgiving my sins and giving me eternal life. Take control of the throne of my life. Make me the kind of person You want me to be.*[47]

Once this prayer has been prayed, the following passages offer assurance about life with Christ:

- Revelation 3:20
- 1 John 5:11-13
- Hebrews 13:5
- John 14:21

Those of us who know the Lord are commanded by Him to share the gospel with those who don't know Him. May we do so freely and boldly!

> *Father God, give me a passion for the message of Jesus Christ, the words and the boldness I need to tell it, and an audience who wants to hear it. Holy Spirit, go before me to prepare hearts and help me when I do have an opportunity to share the news of Jesus' life, death, and resurrection. Amen.*

Taking Action

❖ If you have never walked through the process outlined above and prayed the prayer provided, kneel before God and ask Jesus to become the Lord of your life. Then read the Scriptures listed above to confirm your decision.

❖ If you've named Jesus Lord of your life, spend time practicing how you will share the good news with others. Know that sharing starts at home and that sharing happens with how we live, not just what we say.

Reading On

Read the Scriptures listed in today's devotion.

> To be without some of the things you want is an indispensable part of happiness.
>
> — *Bertrand Russell*

A Battle Cry

The present time is of the highest importance—
  it is time to wake up to reality....
The night is nearly over; the day has almost
  dawned...
Let us arm ourselves for the fight of the day!

— *Romans 13:11-12 (Phillips)*

A High Calling

Scripture Reading: Romans 12:9-21

Key Verse: Romans 12:9

Love must be sincere. Hate what is evil; cling to what is good.

———— ❖ ————

Dr. Halbeck, a missionary of the Church of England in the South of Africa, from the top of a neighboring hill saw lepers at work. He noticed two particularly, sowing peas in the field. One had no hands; the other had no feet— these members being wasted away by disease. The one who wanted the hands was carrying the other, who wanted the feet, upon his back; and he again carried the bag of seed, and dropped a pea every now and then, which the other pressed into the ground with his feet: and so they managed the work of one man between the two. Such should be the true union of the members of Christ's body, in which all the members should have the same care one for another.[48]

What a vivid and powerful picture of how the body of Christ is to function. Fundamental to that kind of unity is the love of Jesus. In today's reading, we are called to have a love that is "sincere." In many translations, Romans 12:9

reads, "Let love be without hypocrisy." The term "hypo-crisy" is a stage term which means "acting a part." At the theater, we see people acting and pretending to be characters who aren't at all like who they are in real life. But in our walk of faith, we who are Christians are not to pretend to be someone we're not. Our love for one another is to be sincere, not an act of hypocrisy.

In today's passage, Paul gives other directives on how to live a Christian life that pleases and glorifies God. We are to choose the proper pathway in which to live, and some of these paths are outlined below:

The Path of Sincerity (verse 9)
  Love must be sincere.
  Hate what is evil.
  Cling to what is good.

The Path of Humility (verse 10)
  Be devoted to one another in brotherly love.
  Honor one another above ourselves.

The Path of Passion (verses 11-12)
  Never lack in zeal.
  Keep fervent about serving the Lord.
  Be joyful in hope.
  Be patient in affliction.
  Be faithful in prayer.

The Path of Relationships (verses 13-20)
  Share with God's people who are in need.
  Practice hospitality.
  Bless those who persecute you.
  Do not curse those who hate you.

Rejoice with those who rejoice.
Mourn with those who mourn.
Live in harmony with one another.
Do not be proud.
Be willing to associate with people of low position.
Do not be conceited.
Do not repay anyone evil for evil.
Do what is right in the eyes of the Lord.
Do not take revenge.
If your enemy is hungry, feed him.
If your enemy is thirsty, give him something to
drink.
Do not be overcome by evil, but overcome evil with
good.

God wants you and me to do all these things. No wonder I struggle every day to live the kind of life He wants me to live. In order to put these specifics into practice, I must read the Scripture and pray. Doing so helps me—and will help you—stand strong against Satan who would love to derail me from my goal of living a life that pleases and glorifies God.

Father God, here I am. Use me for Your kingdom. Teach me Your way of love. Fill me with Your love so that I may be willing to carry a brother or sister who needs my help—and help me to receive Your love when I need to be carried. It's a privilege to be called Your child. May I live a life worthy of that calling, a life that truly glorifies You. Amen.

Taking Action

❖ Choose six of the directives from the above list. Beside each one, note what you are going to do today and this week to live it out.

❖ Now write those six directives on an index card. Carry them with you as reminders of the goals you've set for yourself. Better yet, memorize them.

Reading on

Proverbs 6:16-19   Philippians 4:8

The steadfast of mind Thou wilt keep in perfect peace, because he trusts in Thee.

— *Isaiah 26:3*

Notes

1. Written by Dennis E. Hensley. Copyright 1967, renewed 1991 by Dennis E. Hensley. Used by permission.
2. Charles R. Swindoll and Lee Hough, *You and Your Child* (Nashville, TN: Thomas Nelson Publishers, 1977), a study guide to accompany a series of topics on this subject, 1993, p. 33.
3. George E. Young, *For My Son* (Phoenix, AZ: Young Interests, Inc., n.d.), p. 12. Quotes on page 29 (*For My Son*), page 151 (*For My Son*), and page 173 (*For My Daughter*) also used by permission.
4. Based on Greg Laurie, *New Believer's Growth Book* (Riverside, CA: Harvest Ministries, 1985), p. 8.
5. Source unknown.
6. Adapted from Stephen R. Covey, *The Seven Habits of Highly Effective People* (New York: Simon and Schuster, 1989).
7. Robert Fulghum, *All I Really Need to Know I Learned in Kindergarten* (New York: Ballantine Books, 1986), pp. 29-31.
8. Jan Congo, *Free to Be God's Woman* (Ventura, CA: Regal Books, 1985), adapted from p. 94.
9. Larry Crabb, *The Marriage Builder* (Grand Rapids, MI: Zondervan, 1982), p. 22.
10. Randy Phillips in *Seven Promises of a Promise Keeper*, edited and published by Focus on the Family. Copyright © 1994, Promise Keepers. All rights reserved.

International copyright secured. Used by permission.

11. June Hunt, *Seeing Yourself Through God's Eyes* (Grand Rapids, MI: Zondervan Publishing House, 1989), p. 33.

12. Jerry Kirk, "God's Call to Sexual Purity," in *Seven Promises of a Promise Keeper*, edited and published by Focus on the Family. Copyright © 1994, Promise Keepers. All rights reserved. International copyright secured. Used by permission.

13. Patrick Morley, *The Man in the Mirror* (Brentwood, TN: Wolgemuth and Hyatt, 1989), pp. 12-14.

14. Brian Peterson, editor, *New Man*—for Men of Integrity magazine (Boulder, CO: Strang Communications, in cooperation with Promise Keepers), July/August 1994, p. 6.

15. Ibid.

16. Stu Weber, *Tender Warrior* (Sisters, OR: Multnomah Books, 1993), from pages 36-40.

17. Robert Bly, *Iron John* (New York: Vintage Books, 1992), p. 9.

18. Ed and Carol Newenschwander, *Two Friends in Love* (Portland, OR: Multnomah Press, 1986), p. 175.

19. Robert Fulghum, *All I Really Need to Know I Learned in Kindergarten* (New York: Ballantine Books, 1986), pp. 4-6.

20. Bob Benson, *Laughter in the Walls* (Nashville: Impact Books, 1969).

21. Lee Iacocca, *Talking Straight* (New York: Bantam Books, 1988), p. 27.

22. Jerry and Barbara Cook, *Choosing to Love* (Ventura, CA: Regal Books, 1982), pp. 78-80.

23. Paula Yates Sugg, *The Dallas Morning News*, In Memoriam (September 26, 1993), classifieds section.

24. Hank Hanegraaff, *Christianity in Crisis* (Eugene, OR: Harvest House Publishers, 1993), pp. 181-183.

25. James Dobson, *The Strong-Willed Child* (Wheaton, IL: Tyndale House Publishers, 1971), p. 30.

26. James Dobson, *Hide or Seek*, rev. ed. (Old Tappan, NJ: Fleming H. Revell Co., 1979), p. 95.

27. Emilie Barnes, *Things Happen When Women Care* (Eugene, OR: Harvest House Publishers, 1990), pp. 161-162.

28. Dr. R. Newton, *6000 Sermon Illustrations*, edited by Elon Foster (Grand Rapids, MI: Baker Book House, 1992), p. 286.

29. Lee Iacocca, *Talking Straight* (A Bantam Book: New York, 1988), p. 17.

30. Gigi Graham Tchividjian, *Women's Devotional Bible*, *NIV Version* (Grand Rapids, MI: The Zondervan Corporation, 1990), p. 1307.

31. Bruce Narramore, *You're Someone Special* (Grand Rapids, MI: The Zondervan Corporation, 1978), adapted from pp. 61-62.

32. Ibid., adapted from pp. 85-86.

33. Stu Weber, *Tender Warrior* (Sisters, OR: Multnomah Books, 1993), adapted from pp. 54-57.

34. Books by Marilyn Willett Heavilin (published by Thomas Nelson): *Roses in December; Becoming a Woman of Honor; When Your Dreams Die; December's Song; I'm Listening, Lord.*

35. *6000 Sermon Illustrations*, edited by Elon Foster (Grand Rapids, MI: Baker Book House, 1992), p. 286.

36. Robert Fulghum, *All I Really Need to Know I Learned in Kindergarten* (New York: Ballantine Books, 1986), pp. 4-6.
37. Reproduced from the original in the Shaker Collection.
38. Alan Loy McGinnis, *The Friendship Factor* (Minneapolis, MN: Augsburg, 1979), p. 23.
39. Gary J. Oliver, Ph.D., "Black-and-White Living in a Gray World" in *Seven Promises of a Promise Keeper*, edited and published by Focus on the Family. Copyright © 1994, Promise Keepers. All rights reserved. International copyright secured. Used by permission.
40. Ibid., pp. 85-90.
41. Ibid.
42. Lee Iacocca, *Talking Straight* (New York: Bantam Books, 1988), p. 67.
43. Robert G. Schuller, *Self-Esteem, The New Reformation* (Waco, TX: Word Publishing, 1982), pp. 17-18.
44. Marshall H. Hart in *Home Life Magazine* (date unknown).
45. Patrick Morley, *The Man in the Mirror* (Brentwood, TN: Wolgemuth and Hyatt, 1989), pp. 5-7.
46. Lee Iacocca, *Talking Straight* (New York: Bantam Books, 1988), p. 69
47. Bill Bright, *Four Spiritual Laws* (San Bernardino, CA: Campus Crusade for Christ, Inc., 1965), p. 10.
48. *6000 Sermon Illustrations*, edited by Elon Foster (Grand Rapids, MI: Baker Book House, 1992), p. 309.

For more information regarding speaking engagements and additional material, please send a self-addressed stamped envelope to:

More Hours In My Day
2838 Rumsey Drive
Riverside, CA 92506

Other Good
Harvest House Reading

WHAT MAKES A MAN FEEL LOVED
by *Bob Barnes*

Women want exciting, more intimate relationships with the men in their lives. *What Makes a Man Feel Loved* gives wives a unique opportunity to discover what their men think about—priorities, desires, and approaches to difficult situations. Drawing from 42 years of marriage to popular author Emilie Barnes, Bob Barnes' personal (often humorous) experiences and sound biblical principles give women insightful, practical advice that will improve a wife's understanding of the man she loves.

THE 15-MINUTE MONEY MANAGER
by *Bob & Emilie Barnes*

At last, a money-management book for busy people! Watch your finances come into focus as you apply the authors' proven 15-minute principle: Invest a small amount of time and make a big difference. Sixty-two short, quick-reading chapters have hundreds of ready-to-use ideas that will help you manage your money.

ETERNAL IMPACT
by *Phil Downer*

Every man dreams of leaving a legacy. Popular speaker and author Phil Downer reveals how men can leave an eternal legacy through mentoring—sharing with other men Christ's role in marriage, fathering, and relationships. *Eternal Impact* offers men a realistic, step-by-step mentoring guide filled with dynamic examples of discipleship in action, straightforward advice, and genuine openness.

LET HER KNOW YOU LOVE HER
by *Bill Farrel*

What man couldn't use some encouragement in romancing his wife? This little book of romance especially for men contains numerous creative, encouraging ways for husbands to romance the leading lady in their lives.